Praise for

The Real Win

"Colt McCoy and Matt Carter have joined arms to lead men to win. Not just win in athletics or careers, but to win in life. The pages of this book are packed with inspirational words and practical guidance. I heartily recommend it."

—MAX LUCADO, pastor and best-selling author

"*The Real Win: Pursuing God's Plan for Authentic Success* is a really good book. It is honest, transparent, convicting, challenging, and instructive. It makes plain what it really means to 'be the man!' Colt McCoy and Matt Carter invite men to a higher and greater calling as they follow hard after the real man's man, Jesus of Nazareth."

—DANIEL L. AKIN, president of Southeastern Baptist
Theological Seminary

"Men hate asking for directions a little more than they hate to read. It isn't that we can't read; it's just that we need something that keeps our interest and gives us practical help. Welcome to that book. *The Real Win* will help you grow in your faith so that you can be the man God has called you to be."

—DARRIN PATRICK, lead pastor of The Journey

"A gut-wrenching, soul-piercing book that wrestles honestly with questions every man asks and emotions every man feels, whether he ever admits it or not. I will recommend this book to all the men in my church. You won't be able to put it down."

—J. D. GREEAR, author of *Stop Asking Jesus into Your Heart:
How to Know for Sure You Are Saved* and *Gospel: Recovering
the Power That Made Christianity Revolutionary*

"A wonderful and raw work that gets to the heart of all the areas in which men have historically struggled. This book is immensely valuable, not because it points men to success, but because it points men to Jesus and practically walks through how to win by seeking Him in every area of life."

—NATHAN LINO, senior pastor of Northeast Houston
Baptist Church

"I can't speak highly enough about the way this book addresses manhood in our culture. Biblically challenging and radically applicable, it honestly addresses the deepest longings and fears a man faces."

—MATT CHANDLER, author of *The Explicit Gospel*
and *Creature of the Word*

"This is not your typical formula for a book on success and manhood. By humbly and honestly walking through their failures, Matt Carter and Colt McCoy teach the difficult truths we face as men and leaders. I have great hope that through this book, more and more men will begin to see their struggles in marriage, career, and family as a way to point them to the ultimate picture of success: Jesus Christ."

—BRAD LOMENICK, executive director and key visionary
of Catalyst

"As a young man fresh out of college, I know I'm going to chase something with the rest of my life. *The Real Win* helps me lock in on exactly what that should be. This book identifies what's truly satisfying, what's worthy of being chased. I'm in for the win."

—CORY COTTON, cofounder of Dude Perfect and author of *Go Big*

"We live in a world full of scoreboards. Matt and Colt have experienced both wins and losses, and I've seen them both want God more than all of it. They are men who fight well, and they will lead you to fight well. This is worth it. In *The Real Win*, Matt and Colt will move you from a life of striving to one of fulfillment, living for the God who has already won the ultimate victory."

—JENNIE ALLEN, Bible teacher and author of *Anything*

THE REAL
WIN

COLT McCOY
MATT CARTER

with Marcus Brotherton

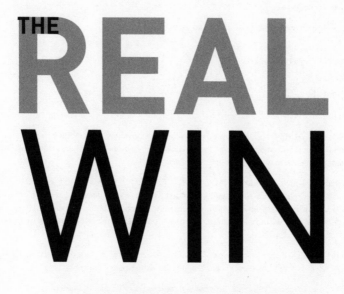

THE
REAL
WIN

Pursuing God's Plan
for Authentic Success

MULTNOMAH
BOOKS

THE REAL WIN
PUBLISHED BY MULTNOMAH BOOKS
12265 Oracle Boulevard, Suite 200
Colorado Springs, Colorado 80921

Italics in Scripture quotations reflect the author's added emphasis.

Trade Paperback ISBN 978-1-60142-484-6
Hardcover ISBN 978-1-60142-482-2
eBook ISBN 978-1-60142-483-9

Cover design by Mark Ford

Published in the United States by WaterBrook Multnomah, an imprint of the Crown Publishing Group, a division of Random House LLC, New York, a Penguin Random House Company.

MULTNOMAH and its mountain colophon are registered trademarks of Random House LLC.

The Library of Congress has catalogued the hardcover edition as follows:
McCoy, Colt.
    The real win : a man's quest for authentic success / Colt McCoy and Matt Carter.
        pages cm
    Includes bibliographical references.
    ISBN 978-1-60142-482-2—ISBN 978-1-60142-483-9 (electronic)
    1. Success—Religious aspects—Christianity. I. Title.
    BV4598.3.M43 2013
    248.8'42—dc23

                                                        2013002167

Printed in the United States of America
2014—First Trade Paperback Edition

10 9 8 7 6 5 4 3 2 1

SPECIAL SALES
Most WaterBrook Multnomah books are available at special quantity discounts when purchased in bulk by corporations, organizations, and special-interest groups. Custom imprinting or excerpting can also be done to fit special needs. For information, please e-mail SpecialMarkets@WaterBrookMultnomah.com or call 1-800-603-7051.

Colt: To my wife, Rachel. It's a joy living life with you every day. May we continue to grow stronger in the Lord together each moment He allows.

Matt: For my wife, Jennifer, who has walked beside me on my journey to manhood. Your love for Jesus is inspiring. Your love for me is humbling.

Trust in the Lᴏʀᴅ forever,
  for the Lᴏʀᴅ Gᴏᴅ is an everlasting rock.

Iꜱᴀɪᴀʜ 26:4, ᴇꜱᴠ

CONTENTS

It's Time to Redefine Winning

Guys, quick! Can you name who won last year's...

- Super Bowl?
- World Series?
- NBA Finals?
- Daytona 500?
- PGA Tour Championship?

How did you do?

If you're like a lot of guys, you're probably surprised by how few of the winners you can recall, especially considering what a big deal those championships felt like to a lot of people at the time.

Inside each man is a desire to set goals and achieve them, to get ahead and finish strong. And God Himself put a desire within us to drive hard and live with excellence. But things can go terribly wrong as we pursue our goals, can't they?

So many men start out to achieve what they think is the real win, but at the end of their lives they feel a sense of defeat, even though they achieved everything they set out to win. They think they're achieving what matters most in the long run, but it doesn't pan out the way they had hoped. Or they find that their goals disappoint them, or their accomplishments are quickly forgotten, or they achieve their goals but destroy their marriages and families in the process, or they never fulfill their destinies and end up frustrated, angry, hurt, and cynical. What then?

Lately, the two of us have been doing a lot of thinking about what constitutes authentic success for a man.

RAISED TO BE A WINNER

Since boyhood, I (Colt) have been trained to win. I have wanted to win and have been expected to win. I even grew up thinking that if I did everything right, God would make sure I won.

A few years back, when I graduated from college, I ended up being the winningest quarterback in college football history. (That record's been broken now, but it felt good to achieve that goal at the time.) Yet even with all those successes, I still came up short with my goals and didn't achieve a couple of big wins I really wanted. And that hurt. I've gone on to play in the NFL, where I've had some successes as well as some challenges. My professional story is still being lived out even as we're writing this book.[1]

I get that most men don't play professional sports for a living. And some men reading this book aren't even football fans. But I'm pretty sure you can relate to my story, because no matter what you do for a living or how you like to spend your free time, all of us can relate to this: we hate to lose. All of us want to be a success, in one way or another. That's why we want to talk about what *real* winning—winning according to God's definition of success—means, and how you can build a life as a man who makes winning a sure thing.

> We want to talk about what real winning— winning according to God's definition of success—means, and how you can build a life as a man who makes winning a sure thing.

I'm still learning a lot as I go along, and that's one of the reasons I'm writing this book along with my friend and pastor, Matt Carter.

Winning or Losing?

Some people think of pastors as guys who don't have a competitive drive, who don't have a desire to succeed like everybody else. But I (Matt) am wired like every other man reading this book. I know what it's like to want to win. The church I planted started with a core group of fifteen people and now has more than eight thousand active attenders. Only God can bring dead souls to life, and He gets every bit of the glory for what's gone right at my church. But still, on my end there was a lot of work to do, and I know what it's like to drive hard. When it came to planting Austin Stone Community Church, humanly speaking, I did succeed.[2]

But I've also learned a thing or two about losing in the process. For one thing, I've faced death (more about that later). For another, I've faced a crisis in my marriage—a crisis that showed me how close I had come to losing everything when I actually thought I was winning. Through these events and many more, I've realized that if you're going to win in the short time you have here on earth, you have to redefine success. You have to make sure you're winning, not according to human standards, but according to God's.

Today Colt and I want to deliver a cautionary tale for men: If the pursuit of God and trusting Him fully isn't at the core of your life, then it's going to be impossible for you to really win. In fact, in every way that really matters, *you'll lose.* That's what we want to talk about in this book. What does true success for a man, particularly a follower of Christ, look like?

It's been great to work on this book with my good friend Colt. Even though I'm an Aggie and he's a Longhorn, and the two don't normally get along (that's an understatement!), we've developed a great respect for each other over the years. Colt's got a lot of insights in this area. He's a man of wisdom well beyond his years.

Sometimes in this book Colt will be talking to you directly, and sometimes I will be, but every part of the message between these book covers is something that we both fully own and that we can't wait to share with you.

This Is for You

If you're concerned about winning at what really counts before your life on this earth is done, then this book is for you. Maybe you've had some successes, maybe *many* successes (though probably not as many as you would have liked), but you still have a nagging sense that what you're working so hard for may not be the right goal after all, at least not entirely. All of us know the awkward feeling when we start to wonder if we've got our ladder up against the wrong wall. As a Christ follower, you want whatever God wants for you, because deep inside you sense that that's where the real win for you must lie. We respect your desire. And we believe God does too. But what you *do* with that desire is what really matters.

Your quest for authentic success starts here.

Now, if you're a woman and you're checking out this book to see what it's got to say, no need to feel guilty about peeking! There are no secrets here, only revelations from the Word of God and the lives of men. Maybe you have a son, a husband, or some other important male in your life, and you want to know how to better encourage him in his pursuit of godly manhood. That's great—this book will open your eyes as well as his. Share with him the insights you read here, or propose that the two of you read the book together and discuss it.

> All of us know the awkward feeling when we start to wonder if we've got our ladder up against the wrong wall.

And that brings us to another opportunity. You see, we need to acknowledge that men have a tendency to remain in their own isolated silos, trying to work on their problems all alone. So, male reader, while you *can* read this book alone and try to apply it to your life individually, we encourage you to read it and talk it through with others, especially a group of men you can trust. Use the study guide at the back of the book with a male friend, with your mentor, in a men's small group, on a men's retreat, or in any other setting where you can be honest with some other guys. Iron sharpens iron, and if we've been getting spiritually dull, we can help each other get our edge back.

Our promise to you is this: the teachings in this book are based on biblical principles, and if you learn and pursue God's way of doing things, your definition of success will change in the key areas of your life for all the seasons of your life. We want to help you win the way God intended, because it's the only way that lasts.

If that sounds promising to you, then turn the page.

Transformed by Trust

*The real win is trusting God to lead
you into the life He wants you to have.*

> You keep him in perfect peace whose mind is
> stayed on you.
>
> —Isaiah 26:3, ESV

What do you want in life more than anything else?

Can you picture it? Be completely honest. What do you think about the most, dream about, plan for, and strive the hardest to gain?

If you're a Christian, resist the noble urge to answer "to follow Christ" too quickly. That might genuinely be the case, and we certainly encourage you in that direction. But if you're like most men, your goals might be more mixed, more earthly, even if you are a Christian.

What you want more than anything else might be more along the lines of…

- having a great job;
- living an adventurous life;
- being married to the hottest, most understanding woman you know;

- driving the right car and living in the right house;
- having fun with your friends or family;
- climbing the ladder and succeeding in business;
- being financially secure;
- having people respect you; or
- doing something important, maybe even changing the world.

For too many of us, whether or not we would ever come right out and say it, those are our definitions of success. None of these goals are wrong, not if they're seen in the proper perspective. But what we've discovered is that so many men start out to win what they most want but in the end don't get it. Or they think they're achieving what matters most, but in the long run life doesn't pan out the way they'd hoped. What happens then?

> Who you trust and who you serve. Those two decisions change everything for a man.

If we're truly going to succeed, most of us need to redefine success. The real win for a man is built on two simple but strategic components—who you trust and who you serve. Those two decisions change everything for a man. And that's what we're going to explore more in the pages to come. Pursuing the true win takes resolve, and the decision to shoot for it is a choice you make more than once. It takes courage, determination, and faith, and it certainly isn't always easy.

Take it from us. We've both learned the hard way.

MATT'S STORY

In May 2005, I (Matt) was thirty-one years old, and life was going great. I was happily married to my wife, Jenn. We had three healthy young children. The church I had planted three years prior was growing fast and was already up to about a thousand people.

Then one night—completely out of the blue—I began to have massive pains in my stomach. I was taken to the hospital for an emergency appendec-tomy, stayed in the hospital overnight, and was released. Problem solved. Or so I thought.

A couple of days later I was sitting at my desk at work, and I got a phone call from my wife. The doctor had told her that they'd found a malignant tumor in my appendix.

Cancer.

It turned out to be a carcinoid tumor of the appendix, a fairly rare type of cancer. The tumors typically start to spread either when they become 2 centi-meters long or if they break through the appendix wall. My tumor was 1.9 centimeters long, and it had already broken through the wall, so this was bad. Doctors told me that if this type of cancer spreads into your lymph nodes, you're done. Chemo doesn't work. Radiation doesn't work. It's a slow-growing cancer, so it takes a few years to kill you, but there's no hope.

To see if the cancer has spread, they test your blood, then they do a CAT scan to see if your lymph nodes are enlarged. I had all these tests, and my blood levels came back abnormally high. That was bad news. Then it turned out my lymph nodes were significantly swollen. Double dose of bad news.

Doctors told me that either the cancer had spread and I was going to die or my blood markers were high because of the original tumor and my nodes were swollen because of the surgery. One option meant death. The other option meant life. The only way to tell which scenario was factual was to wait a few months to see if my blood markers would go down. The second option was slim. As a thirty-one-year-old man, I was preparing to die.

For the next three months, I sat on pins and needles, thinking, hoping, praying. I experienced every dark emotion imaginable. What would happen to my wife and children? What would happen to my church? I struggled to un-derstand why God would allow this to happen to me.

I began to take careful inventory of my life. Some of the first verses of Scripture I read during those days were from Jeremiah 2, where God talks about people who have forsaken Him and tried to do life on their own. I knew in my heart that in so many ways those verses described me. A friend of mine who had gone through a similar trial said these words about his experience: "The Lord brought me into the desert to win my heart." That pretty much summed up what I was experiencing. I knew that whether I lived or died, God was definitely trying to get my attention. Honestly, I had some unconfessed sin in my life and was pursuing a thousand other things besides Jesus.

Then one day, in the midst of my wrestling with God, I got a phone call from a longtime friend, Neil McClendon, a pastor in Houston.

"Matt," he said with his characteristic gravelly voice, "I was spending time with the Lord this morning, and you came to mind. I believe I've got a message from God for you."

"Okay, I'm listening." My heart raced in my chest. I had no idea what Neil was going to say.

"Matt, I don't know whether you're going to live or die. But here's the message: the Lord wants you to live with unction."

" 'Unction'? What does that mean?"

"Matt, it means holy urgency. That's how God wants you to live."

"I still don't get it, Neil."

"Read Psalm 39:4–5. Then you'll know." Neil hung up.

I grabbed my Bible and turned to the passage.

Show me, O LORD, my life's end
    and the number of my days;
    let me know how fleeting is my life.
You have made my days a mere handbreadth;
    the span of my years is as nothing before you.
    Each man's life is but a breath. (NIV)

I chewed on that. Ever breathed on a window during a cold winter's day? Did you notice how it fogged up, and then the fog instantly disappeared? That is what the psalmist David is saying the life of man is like. Here for a brief moment, then gone. Why would David ask God to show him the shortness of his life? David knew that when a man grasps how short his life is, he begins to live with a new sense of what's truly important.

After reading that verse, I had my first glimpse of how God was trying to change my heart through the trial I was facing. God wanted me to live with a holy urgency. Live with *unction*. Whether I lived for two more years or five more decades, compared with all eternity my life was short. I needed to live with a sense of life's fleetingness, of how, in the eyes of God, my life was a mere breath. If I truly believed that, it was going to change the way I lived.

WHAT CHANGED FOR ME

Think of it this way. If you knew you were going to die tomorrow, how would you spend your last hours?

- Would you watch reruns on TV or spend every second you could with your family?
- Would you daydream about other women or look your wife straight in the eyes and tell her you love her more than anything?
- Would you bury yourself behind the newspaper or sit down with your kids at dinner and point them to Jesus?
- Would you look at porn? Would you cheat on your taxes or talk negatively about your coworkers? Or engage in any number of the sins that so easily entangle us? Or would you strive for Jesus as never before, knowing that you would soon see Him face to face?
- Would you read your Bible and pray and live each moment you have left in the conscious presence of God?

God was showing me that there is a direct connection between understanding how short my life is and the urgency in which I would live that life. God wanted to teach me how to number my days, how to know time was short, and how not to live in vain. God wanted me to live with holy urgency.

It's a hard lesson to learn. Three months went by, and it was time for my next round of tests. The night before my tests, I paced around my bedroom. I vented to Jenn about how frustrated I was that I'd done everything I knew how to do, I'd confessed every sin that I'd ever committed, yet God was still not freeing me from this trial. Finally, out of anxiety, exhaustion, and nervousness, I lost my cool and yelled at the top of my lungs, "Jennifer, what does God want from me? I've done everything I can think of. What is He trying to teach me?"

Calmly, my wife looked at me and said, "Matt, I don't know what God's trying to teach you. But I know this: He wants you to *trust Him.*"

The next day I went to the cancer ward and sat in the waiting room, surrounded by dying people. My Bible in my hands, I began reading the story of Jesus on the cross. While Jesus was up there, some guy started mocking Him, saying things like "Hey, I thought You trusted God. Why are You on this cross, then? Why don't You *trust Him* to get You off the cross?" (see Matthew 27:40–43). Right in front of me were the two words my wife had said the night before: *trust Him.* And while I was reading, the answer to why I was still in a place of difficulty hit me like a bolt of lightning. The Holy Spirit impressed these words on my heart so strongly: *Sometimes trusting in God means you don't get to get off the cross.*

> Sometimes trusting God means you don't get to climb down from your cross.

That was the start of my beginning to understand this strange win that God was pointing me to. When Jesus was on the cross, He *was* fully trusting God. The cross didn't look like a win that most people would imagine for someone who was going to save the world. Yet the cross is still exactly what God wanted for Jesus. The nails were in Jesus's hands for a reason.

Something turned in my heart, and I realized it was true that sometimes trusting God means you don't get to climb down from your cross. Meaning, whatever difficulty you're bearing, whatever goal you're not achieving, staying in that difficulty might be a part of God's perfect plan for your life. Losing in the eyes of the world just might be success in the eyes of God.

After my second round of tests were done, I went back to my office, got on my knees, looked up at the ceiling, and prayed, "Lord, if it's Your will for me to die, I trust You." I'd said this to Him before, but this was the first time I really meant it. I fully surrendered right then. I let go. A peace and confidence came over me like I'd never felt before. Without a shadow of a doubt, I knew that every moment of my life was in God's hands.

The next day a phone call came. My blood work was normal. My lymph nodes were normal. All my test results were normal. There was no sign of cancer anywhere. As of the writing of this book, I've been completely cancer-free for seven years. I don't know if God healed me miraculously or if I'd never had any more cancer than the appendix tumor. And I'm not saying that if you trust God, He'll solve your problems in the same way my cancer was taken away from me. But this is what I know for sure: God brought me to a place where I said, "If You want to keep me on the cross, then I trust You."

Can you say that about your life? No matter what happens—good or bad—can you fully trust God? That's the truth that we men so desperately need to learn.

Yes, we want to succeed. We want so badly to reach our goals, and our goals are not wrong at all. In fact, they're usually very good goals. But if you don't achieve what you want to, can you still say that you trust God no matter what?

That's a question Colt and I worked on together for more than a year.

Colt's Story

For my whole life, I've been hard-wired to win.

If you're a boy growing up in Texas with a football in your hands, it's your dream to play at the University of Texas for Coach Mack Brown. It's your dream to lead your team to the National Championship. And it's your dream to win the Heisman.

By the time I was a junior in college, I'd achieved a lot of that dream. It was 2008 and I was quarterback for the University of Texas Longhorns. We were ranked number one in several polls. We went through a long stretch of the season where we beat some of the best college football teams in the country.

Then we came to a big game that would likely determine whether we would go to the BCS National Championship or not. It was toward the end of a tough stretch of conference games, we were up against Texas Tech, and both sides fought hard all game long. Finally, with the clock ticking, we scored to take the lead, 33–32. There were eighty-nine seconds left in the game. We kicked off to Tech, and they threw two long throws down the field. They ended up scoring on the last play of the game. I couldn't believe it! One second stood on the clock. We lost the game and didn't go to the National Championship.

One dream lost.

Then came the Heisman. The Heisman is the longest-standing award and one of the most prestigious in college football. The award is voted upon strictly by media members. Winning the Heisman is like being voted college football's most valuable player. I'd won other awards, lots of them, including being a consensus All-American for two years (meaning the Associated Press had voted me best college quarterback two years in a row). But in the back of my mind, I thought that for myself and for my teammates it would be an amazing honor to win the Heisman.

That same year, as a junior, I went to the Heisman award ceremonies in New York City. I was up against two other players: Sam Bradford, the accurate and very successful quarterback from Oklahoma, and Tim Tebow, Florida's quarterback who had won the Heisman the year before. All three of us had had strong seasons. Any of us could emerge the victor.

When the ballots were counted, Tim came in third, Sam won the Heisman, and I came in second. Being runner-up for the Heisman might sound good, but it was actually a huge disappointment to me. It's hard to fully explain, but ask yourself this: Who *lost* last year's Super Bowl? Can you remember the team that didn't win? That's what it felt for me to be runner-up for the Heisman—not good enough. I was just as disappointed for my teammates and coaches and fans as I was for myself.

Two dreams lost.

So the stakes were really raised in 2009. I decided to come back for my senior year after a couple of weeks of seriously contemplating entering the NFL draft. I was well within reach of one last shot at winning the Heisman, and more importantly, my team had one last shot at winning the National Championship. My final year as a college player would be my last chance to achieve what I'd been working toward all my life.

> Ask yourself this: Who lost last year's Super Bowl? Can you remember the team that didn't win?

Matt began to disciple me just before the start of that year. We met almost every week in his office, poring through Scriptures together and praying. The things I was telling Matt about myself felt kind of trivial at first. My "problems" were nothing compared to his having cancer. I wasn't dying of a life-threatening disease. I just wasn't winning how I wanted to win. But Matt showed me that the level of difficulty a person faces isn't the issue. Everybody encounters problems in life in the pursuit of his goals, and the problems are valid to each person. No matter what difficulty you're facing, God wants you to trust Him through it.

For me, that proved easier said than done. I'd say, "Oh yeah, Matt, I know I need to trust in God." But then when something bad happened, I'd still get frustrated because God wasn't blessing me in the way I thought I needed to be blessed.

For example, a few weeks after Matt first told me his cancer story, I threw an interception during a big game and it folded me up inside. Matt pulled me aside and said, "Colt, God sometimes has us go through difficult things because He's trying to get us to trust Him. It doesn't mean you don't go out and play your hardest. It doesn't mean you don't strive for the best. It doesn't mean you don't work as for the Lord. But it does mean that when bad things happen, you're not shaken; you trust."

I took Matt's words to heart. I didn't need to give up my quest to win. In fact, the verse that he was alluding to—Colossians 3:23—had been my favorite verse for years. As a matter of fact, I put that verse under my name every time I sign my name for an autograph. It says, "Whatever you do, work heartily, as for the Lord and not for men" (ESV). In light of this verse, every day I showed up for practice, every game I played, I was going to do everything I could physically, mentally, and spiritually with the gifts God has given me, and yet still remember that my life was in God's hands, regardless of what came about. I still live that way today.

But it was awhile before my decision to fully trust God took hold. At one point Matt asked me directly, "Colt, you always point to the sky and give God glory when you throw a touchdown or your team wins. But have you come to the place where, if you don't achieve your goals, you can still point your index finger up at heaven and say, 'God, I trust You'?"

I wanted to do this. I truly did. But I wasn't sure if I was genuinely there yet.

I had yet to be tested.

What Changed for Me

In December 2009 I went to New York again as one of the candidates for the Heisman award—my second year in a row. But I returned to the awards ceremony only to see the trophy handed to Mark Ingram, Alabama's star running back. Toby Gerhart of Stanford came in second, and I came in third. It was the closest points race since 1985.

One dream lost—again.

I kept pressing on. At the end of the regular season, Texas beat Texas A&M, and my team was headed to the BCS National Championship. This was my absolute final shot at winning the college football championship.

The National Championship was played in California. We traveled there, but my body was still on Texas time. So the evening before the game and all game day prior to kickoff, I had a lot of time to think and prepare. We were the underdogs, but I was confident we could win. By then I'd played with my team for four years. I was the leader of the team, and I knew how everyone ticked. We were all ready. It was on. I was going to do all I could to put our team in a position to win. I'd never been more prepared going into any game as I was that day.

As I was reading my Bible, I came across Isaiah 26:3–4.

> You keep him in perfect peace
>> whose mind is stayed on you,
>> because he trusts in you.
> Trust in the LORD forever,
>> for the LORD GOD is an everlasting rock. (ESV)

Go ahead and take the time to read that verse again.

That passage is what I meditated on going into the 2009 National Championship, and it's become the passage that undergirds what my life is about today. Really, the themes found in that passage are what this book is about too. I didn't know it just then, but that verse would become incredibly important to me. It works best if Matt and I alternate to tell you this next bit of the story.

Matt:

The National Championship began. It was the Longhorns versus the number-one-ranked University of Alabama. I was watching the game on TV at home in Austin, and during UT's first possession, Colt absolutely dominated the opponent. I mean, Colt drove his team down the field like there was nobody playing on defense. The game was off to an incredible start, and the National Championship looked well within reach. I was shouting at the TV, urging Colt on. Colt and I had been praying for this moment all year, and nothing could stop this kid.

I had to blink twice when I saw it happen. It was still the first main drive down the field, and Colt's team was on the opponent's five-yard line. They were ready to score. The ball was snapped, and from the blindside a 296-pound defensive lineman broke free and plowed into Colt's shoulder, and Colt went down. Colt had been hit harder than that dozens of times before. He should have bounced back up, shaken it off, and run back to join his team in the huddle.

But this time when Colt stood up, something was wrong.

Colt's arm hung at his side, limp. It looked lifeless. I could see it on camera. Colt wasn't moving it. And a thought struck me: *What happens next has the potential to define Colt's life for a long time to come.*

Colt:

It had been a beautiful first drive. I had completed five out of five passes up to the point of the hit. We were marching down the field and just about to score. Then—*bam!*

I wasn't really in pain. A ton of adrenaline was still coursing through my body. Instead of joining my team in the huddle, I jogged toward the sideline. More than anything, I was in shock, asking, "What is this? What's going on?" The lineman had come off the edge and hit me square on the shoulder of my throwing arm. My whole arm from the shoulder down to my hand was completely numb. I couldn't raise my arm. I couldn't feel my fingers. I couldn't grip anything. Maybe you've felt the sensation that happens when you sleep on your arm, wake up, and your arm is there but it's heavy and dead. That's what I felt.

So I sat on the bench, and Coach Brown replaced me with my backup, freshman Garrett Gilbert. The trainers began to work on me, and I sat there completely focused on everything the trainers were trying to do for me. I kept thinking, *Surely this is going to come back. Surely!* My right arm was what had gotten me to where I was that day. But everything in my arm stayed silent.

If it had been my left arm, I would have kept playing. If it had been my ankle, I would have taped it up and gone back on the field. But a quarterback without his throwing arm is useless.

I walked back to the locker room with the trainers and kept trying. I put ice all over my shoulder. They took x-rays, trying to figure out what was wrong so they could wake it up. There was no reaction. Thirty minutes went by. Remember, this was my last game in a college uniform. This was everything.

There hadn't been a quarterback playing at the University of Texas besides me for the past four years. But the truth slowly sank in. I was physically spent, emotionally spent. I was done.

> I would have done anything for those guys in that room, and they knew that.

Halftime rolled around, and Alabama was beating us 24–6. The atmosphere in our locker room was dispirited, to say the least. By this time, most of my team knew I wasn't coming back in the game. I got up anyway and tried to encourage my team the best I could. I would have done anything for those guys in that room, and they knew that.

The trainers were calling it a "nerve impingement," and there was nothing they could do for it. They told me to hop in the showers and get my street clothes back on. But I was having none of that. I thought, *No way. I'm going to put my pads back on, strap my shoes back on, and go out to the bench with a headset on. If there's any way my arm comes back to life with any amount of time left in the game, I'm going back in.* For the second half of the game, I stood on the sidelines and did my best to cheer on the team. That was all I could do. (It would be three more weeks before the feeling returned.)

We lost. Alabama won the National Championship 37–21. It was a tough, tough thing to stand there watching, knowing I couldn't do anything. It was tough afterward to listen to all the media speculation and all the armchair quarterbacks—people who said I didn't want to play because I was more concerned with the NFL draft status. (If you know me, you know that thought never even crossed my mind. Ever. I could have left for the NFL the year before. I had just as much opportunity then and possibly would have been drafted higher than I eventually was.)

Right after the game was over, I walked back to the locker room. The heaviest disappointment I'd ever felt in my life descended on me. I knew what the game meant to me, my teammates, my coaches, and the fans. Lisa Salters, the sideline reporter for ABC, tugged at the corner of my jersey and asked for an interview. A cameraman stood next to her. I nodded, and the next thing I heard was Lisa saying, "I'm with Texas quarterback Colt McCoy. Colt, what was it like for you to watch this game—the last game in uniform—from the sideline?"[1]

> Words came out of my mouth that I now know could have only come from an unseen source.

I started to answer twice, stammering, "I... I..." I had no words of my own just then.

I paused to gather myself. Then words came out of my mouth that I now know could have only come from an unseen source.

Matt:

When Colt went down, I immediately started praying, "Lord, let him back in the game." I was begging God, wrestling with the same issues of trust, asking, "What in the world are You doing? Don't You know how huge this is, God?"

Then the report came saying Colt wasn't getting back in the game.

For a moment I sat there in front of my TV, completely deflated. Then it hit me like a ton of bricks: *No, for reasons we'll never fully understand, what's happening at this exact moment is part of God's perfect plan. This moment is what God has been preparing Colt for all year long.*

Instead of worrying, I trusted God and prayed that Colt would do the same.

I knew there was going to be a postgame interview with Colt, and I began to pray, "God, give him the right words to say."

Sure enough, after the game Lisa Salters came on the screen with Colt at her side. A microphone was in his face. I knew this was the moment.

Colt started slowly at first:

"I... I..." He cleared his throat and began again. "I love this game. I have a passion for this game.

"I've done everything I can to contribute to my team, and we made it this far.

"It's unfortunate that I didn't get to play. I would have given everything I had to be out there with my team.

"Congratulations to Alabama.

"I love the way our team fought. Garrett Gilbert stepped in and played as good as he could play. He did a tremendous job..."

Then, as Colt finished speaking, he said one last phrase. It brought me to my feet in my living room. I heard the words and stared at the screen.

Colt:

I said: "I always give God the glory. I never question why things happen the way they do. God is in control of my life, and I know that if nothing else, I am standing on the Rock."

Matt:

I screamed at the top of my lungs. "That's it!"

Colt:

I know those words came to me because of God. They came because I had been meditating on Isaiah 26:3–4 before the game.

God was keeping me in perfect peace because my mind was stayed on Him.

God was my eternal Rock, and although I was hugely disappointed over not winning, my life wasn't going to be shattered. God was still in control.

That's what I told everybody that day, and that's what I had come to truly believe.

Matt:

On national television, with the whole world watching, Colt had just quoted Isaiah 26. Within two seconds of Colt's interview, my phone started going off. I bet it went off a hundred times. Everyone who knew that Colt and I were friends started texting me, saying things like, "Unbelievable," and "God was glorified through that," and "Tell Colt I'm so proud of him," and "That's the coolest thing I've ever heard in my life."

This young man hadn't only given glory to God when he had won, but he just gave glory to God when he had lost the biggest game of his life.

That's what it means to truly win. It means that eternity is always in view. Colt could have been shattered, but instead he stood confidently on the eternal Rock of God.

Colt:

It's true that I was hugely disappointed. If you could imagine what I felt in that moment—my whole life had been built around winning that game. Everything I had spent hours upon hours preparing for was encapsulated in that event.

Yet God chose to use me in that moment of pain and failure to glorify Him. And that was okay with me. Yes, the experience hurt. It was painful. I still have nightmares about it today. I still get upset when I think about it. But that was the route God allowed me to walk down. I know now that things in this life don't always go as planned, but I'm confident that I'm on the journey God wants me to be on, and I'll go where He wants me to go.

The Real Win for You

So that's what this book is about: trusting God in the deepest way possible. This is where the real win in a man's life comes from.

Redefining success is a task for every man, including you. The task isn't always easy, but the rewards pay off in big ways. With God at the core of your life, your life is rock-steady. You don't have to wonder, *Am I committing myself to the right tasks? Am I a part of something that really matters? Am I valuable?* You're not on the shifting sands of your own best notions and efforts; you're built on the Rock. A peace and an assurance like you've never felt before flood your life.

That's the surprising reward of faithfully serving God—absolute confidence. It's not so much a confidence in yourself or your abilities, although that's often a by-product of trusting God. It's a confidence in the righteous character of God Himself. God is good all the time, and God always has our best interests at heart. Trusting God means knowing that our lives are being lived out in the center of His perfect plan.

> That's the surprising reward of faithfully serving God—absolute confidence.

We don't have all of life figured out by any means, and both of us still make as many mistakes as the next guy. But we want to talk to you in the pages ahead about how God has changed our life stories—how by trusting and serving Him wholeheartedly, we've seen Him change our marriages, families, hearts, careers, and lives. Through the truths we've discovered in the Scriptures, we are learning how to be the men God calls us to be.

We invite you to do the same. To learn how to trust God more fully than you ever have before, and then do it. The way of living presented in this book isn't about shining yourself up or pulling yourself up by the bootstraps. It's about a love relationship with Jesus, about grace and not perfection, about following and obeying a God who cares for you, no matter what.

Consider this your personal call to redefine success in your life. When you trust in the Lord as your eternal Rock, you can be absolutely confident no matter life's circumstances.

Achievement vs. Faithfulness

Why are so many men chasing after the wrong kind of success? Because they're not pursuing God's eternal purposes.

[God] has put eternity into man's heart.

—ECCLESIASTES 3:11, ESV

Awhile back I (Matt) was talking with a group of people at a backyard event associated with my church when I noticed a little boy hanging around and looking as if he didn't have anything to do. He was about ten years old, the same age as my daughter, so just to be friendly, I started talking to him. I asked where his dad was.

"On a business trip," the boy said. "He's going to be gone for a couple of weeks."

"Oh, do you miss your dad when he's gone like that?"

"Nah, not really."

I was shocked. "How come?" I asked.

"Well, he's never around, even when he's home. When he is, he's always in his office working. I only see him a few minutes each day. Honestly, he doesn't pay much attention to us."

In less than seven seconds, that boy spoke a mouthful. In fact, it broke my heart. I was expecting to hear the opposite—that he missed his dad greatly. I hope that if I were gone on business and somebody asked my kids if they missed me, they'd say, "Absolutely."

Now I don't know this boy's father, and I don't know the specific circumstances of this family's life. Maybe the boy's father doesn't have a choice to live differently than he's doing right now. Or maybe the boy was just having a bad day and venting about his father being gone.

> We start out to win the way we want to win, but in the end we lose in what really counts.

But what hit me was the face value of the exchange between us. I asked the boy if he missed his father, and the boy said no. If we take the boy's words as he presented them, then something was seriously wrong.

That begs the question: If given the choice, why would any man work so hard and long that it would distance him so severely from his family? Why would a man do that?

I know the answer, and maybe that's why it broke my heart like it did.

The troubling answer comes around to what we were getting at in chapter 1 of this book. We men are born to strive, to compete, to shoot for success. But as we pursue our goals, things can go terribly wrong. We start out to win the way we want to win, but in the end we lose in what really counts. Or we think we're achieving what matters most, but along the way we end up losing what we actually value.

We said before that it all comes down to *Who do you trust?* and *Who do you serve?* In the last chapter we saw how important it is to trust God. Now we can see how vitally important it is to grasp the who-do-you-serve component in redefining success just as soon as we can—and then live to that aim every day. As we begin to sort that out together, let's circle around again to the question, why would a man ignore his family?

I know why only because I've done that.

How I Missed the Mark

As of the writing of this book, Austin Stone Community Church is ten years old. Those ten years have gone by so fast. I can't believe that a decade ago I was just starting this good work. My daughter, Annie, had just been born when we planted the church. And—here's my confession—looking back at that time, I have almost no memories of my sweet little girl's first two years of life.

That fact devastates me. I was so involved with planting my church, so consumed with making sure everything ran smoothly, so absorbed in pursuing my goal and creating a success, that I missed out on an important block of my princess's young life.

Now, my wife is a down-to-earth southern beauty who doesn't pull punches. So she'd tell you that for several years during that time, I flat-out ignored my family. It wasn't that I didn't love my wife and kids; it's just that I was consumed with my job. The church had become a mistress to me. I had a love affair with my career, and it stole my rightful allegiances.

I've since reconciled things with my family and have brought my life more into balance. But the story is a common one, and the question remains: men, in our quest for success and achievement, why do things like this happen?

- Why do some men drive themselves so hard at work that they lose the hearts of their wives and kids? It's possible to still live in the same house with them, but these men have long ago lost their family's hearts.

- Why do some men, in their pursuit of achievement, even men who are normally men of integrity, bend ethical standards in order to succeed in business? They seek position, power, and financial status so highly that they are willing to break the rules. These men gain something they want but lose their integrity in the process.

- Why do some men, in their quest for happiness, find it easy to become discontent in the covenant of marriage? Why, when I do marriage counseling, do I keep hearing this false statement: "I'm just not happy. And I've always been taught that God wants me to be happy above all else"?

- Why do so many men, in a quest for escapism, keep looking at pornography—even when they don't want to?

- Why do young men, in their desire to get the approval and acceptance of others, do things they would normally never do? I see this in the young men who come to me for counseling. They say and do things that are not glorifying to God, simply because they want to be accepted by a group of guys in a fraternity, for instance, or because they want to push physical boundaries with the young women they're dating.

- Why do so many men want so desperately to feel respected and approved? So when a business deal goes wrong, or when somebody says something they don't like, they spiral into fear, dismay, or anger.

A problem exists with this whole way of looking at things. It's true that we men are wired to strive for goals. We want achievement. We want credibility and respect and comfort and release. And we're willing to do just about whatever it takes to reach our goals.

But here's the problem. The things we're so often striving for have a habit of letting us down. They don't deliver the win we hope they will. At the end of the day, those things don't satisfy, whether we get them or not.

The Wrong Way of Looking at Life

I admit that I (Colt) am certainly wired this way.

Toward the end of my college football career, there was a lot of talk about how I was in a good position to be drafted by the NFL, maybe even in the first round. That's certainly something I was striving for. But after my injury in the National Championship game, there were concerns about my shoulder holding up over the long haul. Instead of achieving my goal to be a first-round pick, I ended up getting drafted in the third round.

Now being a third-round pick in the NFL might sound good, but it wasn't all I was hoping for. It's hard to explain fully (and the reason I play football has to do with a lot more than the pay-check), but as one point of compari-son, the provision side of my career ended up taking a hit as a third-round pick compared to the income I would

> My position in the NFL draft sent a clear message to me: I wasn't the man on top.

have made as a first-round pick. Please understand, I'm not complaining about my contract or draft position in any way. It was awesome, and I am happy and grateful to have the opportunity to play in the NFL. Still, when I didn't get drafted in the first round, I felt that same twinge of disappointment I've felt more than once in my career. I felt like this was a situation where God was going to bless me, yet again I was let down. My position in the NFL draft sent a clear message to me: I wasn't the man on top. I had wanted something, and I was working hard to make my goal. But I didn't achieve what I wanted, at least not as fully as I had hoped.

What was tougher to swallow than a lower salary was that when I went to Cleveland, my head coach, Eric Mangini, told me that he'd never had a rookie quarterback play for him, so he wanted my first year to be a "watching and learning year." Our starting quarterback was the talented Jake Delhomme, and his backup was Seneca Wallace, a nine-year veteran of the NFL. That meant I wasn't going to play.

For a guy who had been the starting quarterback at UT, that was disap-pointing. I hadn't missed a start for four years. But now I was going to be watching the game from the sidelines. I needed to work through that discon-tent. I poured myself into training. I decided to prepare for the season like I was the starting quarterback anyway and give all I had to being as prepared as possible.

Here's the principle I learned during that time. Every man has things in his life that he's either pursuing or that he turns to in an attempt to feel fulfilled, valued, satisfied, or relieved. Yet God has designed us in such a way that the only thing that can satisfy that place in us is Him. If a man is relying on the achievement of his goals to make him happy, content, or fulfilled in life, it won't work and he's setting himself up for disappointment.

It goes back to what a man's heart is set on. If my heart had only been set on being a first-round pick or a great starting NFL quarterback, I'd have found myself on the verge of despair more than once. Achievement is still important to me. I get up every day and work my tail off mentally and physically to become a successful quarterback, and I hope that something great is going to happen as I continue in my career. I'm shooting to lead my team well, be the best player I can be, and take my team to the Super Bowl someday.

> I would have never admitted it, but because of my hard work and "obedience," I felt that God owed me success.

But my heart is also set on *more* than those goals. I've realized that being a great quarterback is not my *only* purpose in life. My life's ultimate purpose is about setting my heart on God. That involves serving my wife, leading my family, loving my teammates and coaches, reaching out to my community, and being the best follower of Christ I can be.

That's what a lot of my life story shows so far. Through time, talent, and discipline, I've been fortunate enough to achieve a list of notable athletic achievements. But even these achievements have proved not to be enough. I discovered the hard way that time, talent, and discipline didn't bring about the results I'd hoped for—at least not yet. I would have never admitted it, but because of my hard work and "obedience," I felt that God owed me success. When my achievements faltered and failed, I faced deep discouragement, crises of confidence, and doubts about God.

I think that's a problem every man can identify with—because every man can point to letdowns, personal failures, and defeats in his life. Sooner or later, every man is forced to ask himself the question, If life is supposedly only about achievement, what happens when I don't achieve? The flip side of this win-or-bust mentality is often overlooked—and it's just as dangerous. Some men decide they'll never win, so they do their best to never enter the race. They opt for "safe" careers that leave them dissatisfied.

The bottom line is that there's got to be something other than the approach that says life is all about achievement. And there is. But first we must understand what achievement has become for too many men, including Matt and me. The problem is found in a word we don't use a lot today, but believe me, it's still as big a problem as ever.

This word gets to the root of the problem. And we've got to uncover the root of the problem, see it for what it is, and understand it and confess it before we can go forward and truly succeed.

What's that word?

A Word We've Almost Lost

Idolatry.

That's the root of the problem.

That's what achievement becomes for a lot of men. That's what our goals become to us. That's what all our striving leads to.

Idolatry is a word you don't hear a lot today. When most people hear the world *idolatry,* they think of ancient sacrifices, people bowing down and worshiping golden calves, that sort of thing. Idolatry isn't much of a problem today, people think, because we're not literally slaughtering sheep on the altars of a pagan god. But it turns out idolatry was not just an ancient problem. Idolatry is actually something that every twenty-first-century person struggles with on a daily basis.

Back in the days of the Exodus, Moses climbed to the top of Mount Sinai, where God met him and gave him the Ten Commandments. Notice the very first commandment the Lord gave Moses:

You shall have no other gods before me. You shall not make for yourself a carved image, or any likeness of anything that is in heaven above, or that is in the earth beneath, or that is in the water under the earth. You shall not bow down to them or serve them. (Exodus 20:3–5, ESV)

Since we don't usually carve images to worship anymore, what is the enduring principle here? What is idolatry today? Here's our working definition: *Idolatry is anything you pursue more than you pursue God.*

So ask yourself questions like these. Have you ever…

- desired a job, promotion, or career achievement more than you've desired God?
- wanted the applause or approval of a person or a group of people more than you've wanted God?
- valued something—maybe even a very good thing, like your child, your spouse, or your country—more than you've valued God?
- longed for some sort of status, recognition, position of power, or level of comfort more than you've longed for God?
- pursued something or someone or some goal to a greater degree than you've pursued God?

For both of us (Colt and Matt), the answer in our own lives is yes. We've both allowed our hearts to pursue things or people more than we've pursued God.

We've pursued the wrong win, and we choose now to call it what it is: the sin of idolatry.

How about you?

THE MAN WHO HAS IT ALL

Think of how counterintuitive it seems that God placed idolatry at the top of the list of the Ten Commandments. God tells people not to have idols even before He tells them not to murder other people. Ending another person's life is a horrible thing, but surprisingly it's not the first sin God talks about. Likewise, God talks about idolatry before He tells people not to commit adultery. There are few things in life more destructive to your soul (and to the souls of your wife and children) than adultery. But again, it's not the first sin God talks about.

So why does God talk about idolatry first? It's because idolatry is more present in our hearts than most of us realize. And it is more destructive to our souls than we could ever dream.

Think hard about those two realities.

- Idolatry is present right now in our hearts.
- Idolatry is more destructive to our souls than we could ever dream.

Look way back to King Solomon, who wrote the book of Ecclesiastes. (The struggles that men go through are nothing new.) Solomon spends several chapters of his book explaining that he had access to the best the world had to offer. He had more money than he could ever spend. He ate the best food, drank the best wine, listened to the best music, wore the best clothes, lived in the best houses, slept with the most beautiful women, and became nothing short of the most powerful man in the world. He denied himself nothing that his eyes desired.

> You'd think a man who had it all would be supremely happy.

You'd think a man who had it all would be supremely happy. He'd feel content, satisfied, respected, like he had it all together. But in the end Solomon called it all "vanity." He concluded that there is only one place a man can find true happiness and contentment.

In God.

In fact, that's how God designed it. Look at how Scripture describes this longing:

[God] has put eternity into man's heart, yet so that he cannot find out what God has done from the beginning to the end. (Ecclesiastes 3:11, ESV)

That means that God has placed this thing in your heart and mind called "eternity." It's a different way of saying that God has planted within everybody a longing for the stuff that really matters—the stuff that's eternal.

Who or what is eternal?

God.

God has placed in the heart of every man a longing for Himself, and nothing that isn't Himself, nothing that's not eternal, can fulfill an eternal longing. That's what makes idolatry so destructive. We men spend so much time trying to fulfill the need in our hearts with noneternal things. We may spend our lives pursuing without success something or someone who cannot possibly fill the deepest needs of our heart, or else we actually *do* get this person or thing we want, but when we get it, it doesn't meet that heart longing. It's because a relationship with the living God is what we are really hungering for. And when this realization hits us—that the thing we thought would fulfill us doesn't—then it can crush us. It can bring us to despair.

Hollywood is a great example of the devastation of idolatry. When we look at the stars and celebrities of Hollywood, we may look at them from the outside and see an image of ultimate happiness and fulfillment. They're rich, beautiful, famous, and respected. But pull back the curtains, and almost without exception, they're some of the most miserable people on the planet. Tabloids are filled with stories of celebrity divorces, substance abuse, addiction, depression, and despair. These misfortunes are at epidemic proportions in this subgroup of people.

The reason for this despair is that these people, just like all of us, have idols. But they've actually attained them; they've grasped their goals.

Some had a heart longing for approval and applause. *They got it.*

Some had a heart longing for power and position and status. *They got it.*

Some had a longing to be pursued sexually by beautiful women. *They got it.*

Some had a heart longing for the supposed security and control that comes from wealth. *They got it.*

But did any of their achievements ultimately bring joy, peace, fulfillment, or contentment? No. Plenty of people who get everything they ever wanted find that their lives are train wrecks. And why? Because there is nothing more destructive than spending your life pursuing something that you thought was going to meet the deepest longings of your heart, and one day actually getting it, then realizing that this thing or person does not fill the longings of your heart. And it never will.

That's why so many in Hollywood are miserable. Because they actually got the things they thought would make them happy. And those things didn't deliver. Because those things can't.

When God Gives You Everything

God Himself planted eternity, a longing for the eternal, in every one of our hearts. The only place our hearts will ever find satisfaction for that hunger is not in our achievements, not in winning the National Championship, not in leading a large church, not in a spouse, not in money or financial security, not in position or power or popularity or sex, but in a relationship with the living God.

A part of your heart will never be satisfied with anything under the sun except God. And when you understand that, the tables are turned. Take a look at a verse in the Bible that's easy to grasp at first but much harder to live out.

Delight yourself in the LORD;
And He will give you the desires of your heart. (Psalm 37:4, NASB)

It's easy to give that verse a quick glance and think, *Wow, if I delight myself in the Lord, He'll give me anything I want.* But that's not what God promises in that verse. He's saying, "If and when you delight yourself in the Lord, instead of in all this other stuff and people and experiences, He will give you what your heart truly desires. Instead of your heart being dissatisfied by counterfeit desires, your heart will desire Him." Do you realize the significance of this promise from Scripture?

When you delight yourself in God, you can be poor and yet still experience total and complete contentment.

When you delight yourself in God, you can be single your whole life and yet have the deepest desires of your heart completely satisfied.

When you delight yourself in God, you can be insignificant in the eyes of the world and yet be incredibly important in the eyes of God.

The deepest desires of your heart, at that point, are not a spouse, financial security, or status.

The deepest desire of your heart is God.

The drive to achieve is natural and good, if handled appropriately. But it isn't everything. It isn't why God put you here. Instead the Bible shows us a higher value. The questions become: Are your eyes on Jesus? Are you faithful to His calling? Are you doing your best and leaving the outcomes to God?

> The drive to achieve is natural and good, if handled appropriately. But it isn't everything.

Ultimately, for a man who follows God, success isn't about our achievements. Success is about our faithfulness. If we trust and serve Him, we *will* be successful.

THE ROCK-STEADY MAN

A man once met famed spiritual leader Billy Graham at a dinner and asked him what was the most satisfying part of his life and ministry. The man expected to hear stories about the big revivals, or about being a spiritual advisor to world leaders, or about writing best-selling books that affected lives the world over. But Dr. Graham waved him off and said, "It's none of that. By far the greatest joy of my life has been knowing Jesus—hearing Him speak to me, having Him guide me, sensing His presence. He has been the greatest pleasure of my life."[1]

Dr. Graham delighted himself in the Lord. And the Lord gave him the desire of his heart.

Here's the application. The ultimate point of life is not to achieve things. There's nothing wrong with achievement, but it's not going to satisfy the deepest longings of our hearts. It works both ways. If we achieve all we want, those things won't satisfy us. And if we don't achieve what we want, we won't be satisfied either.

That's why a man needs to be rock-steady. That's why we need to ingest and live out the truth of that portion of Scripture that I (Colt) read right before the National Championship game.

> You keep him in perfect peace
>> whose mind is stayed on you,
>> because he trusts in you.
> Trust in the LORD forever,
>> for the LORD GOD is an everlasting rock. (Isaiah 26:3–4, ESV)

When our minds are firmly fixed on God, then God promises perfect peace. God's not going anywhere. James 1:17 says, "Every good thing given and every perfect gift is from above, coming down from the Father of lights, with whom there is no variation or shifting shadow" (NASB). God is the everlasting Rock. And God promises to us an unshakable confidence based on Him. If your life is based on the everlasting Rock of God, then you can have absolute confidence no matter what happens in life.

For instance:

- If you don't win the National Championship or the Heisman, you can still be absolutely confident that your life is on track.
- If you went to college and got a great job, but then lost it in a recession, you can be absolutely confident that God has a purpose for the difficulty and that your life isn't ruined, even though your résumé might be.
- If you got a life-threatening disease at an early age, you can be absolutely confident God has a plan even in the midst of this extreme hardship.

- If you married your dream girl, but over the years the stresses of
  child rearing and work schedules have put tension in your marriage, you can be confident that God will keep you in perfect
  peace no matter the challenges in your relationship.
- If you've always dreamed of a large-scale ministry, but you're a
  small-town pastor with limited influence year after year, you still
  can be absolutely confident your life is a success because you are
  faithful to God's calling.
- If you're a father and your eyes are on Jesus and the principles in
  God's Word, you can be absolutely confident that God is working
  in the lives of your children.

No matter what life throws at you, it's not your win-loss record that counts.
It's your faithfulness.

Does *faithfulness* sound too much like a church word to you? We think of
the word in core terms of how you authentically live your life. You've already
got the "who" you serve portion figured out—God. Now you decide the "how"
portion of how you live—you commit to going the route of faithfulness. That
means you're...

- unflinching
- determined
- unyielding
- enduring
- steady
- immovable
- unshakable

Are you beginning to see it?

The real win means trusting the Lord and walking with Jesus no matter
what. That kind of faithfulness is possible for any man who follows God with
all his heart. No matter what circumstances threaten him, a faithful man is the
most truly confident man in the room.

You may be reading this chapter and agreeing with it in principle but still thinking something like, *Yeah, but if I can just get this or that, then I'll be happy.* Or, *If I just achieve this or that, then I'll be content.* Or, *If I just experience this or that, then I'll be fulfilled.* That's the longing of your heart talking.

Quit pursuing your idol. Instead, run to Jesus. That's where your real win will be.

In the rest of this book, we'll be exploring the real win in the important parts of a man's life. Here's what you've got ahead of you:

- Pursuing the real win at home (chapters 3–5)
- Pursuing the real win at work (chapters 6–7)
- Pursuing the real win in your character (chapters 8–9)
- Pursuing the real win as you deal with what life throws you over the long term and strive to finish well (chapters 10–11)

We'll be returning to the concept of idolatry when we talk about our work lives. Work, after all, is a big deal to all of us. But before we get to that, we need to look at what's truly the most important arena in a man's life: his family. If you have a wife or children, or if someday you will, you have to expect them to look to you for godly leadership. Are you ready for it?

Willing to Lead

You're the quarterback for your family, and they're looking to you to call the plays.

The head of every man is Christ, the head of a wife is her husband, and the head of Christ is God.

—1 Corinthians 11:3, esv

A television sitcom featured an episode in which a teenage girl and her boyfriend messed up physically, then discovered they were going to have a baby. Naturally, they were both scared and unsure of what to do. One scene showed the young man losing his cool, which didn't help matters. The girl needed the guy to stay calm, be wise, and commit to seeing the situation through. Finally, in an outburst of anger, the girl looked at him and said, "Somewhere inside of that pea brain of yours is a man. Access him!"[1]

As much as a quote like that might get a laugh, there's a ton of truth to it. It's the equivalent of the girl saying, "Take the leadership here," or "Get yourself together, man," or "Wise up!" We guys often have untapped maturity inside us—an "undiscovered man" (for want of a better term)—and our call is to access this maturity and apply it to the situation. We need this maturity when times are hard, if we've made poor decisions and need to make better ones, or simply throughout the normal day-to-day actions of life. The key is not so much that the maturity lies latent within us. It's that it comes from an outside source—God's Word—and we apply it to our lives with courage, grace, and determination.

The Scriptures are clear that God has placed a specific calling on the lives of men: to lead (see the 1 Corinthians verse quoted above, for one example). We're not to be passive. We're not to shift responsibility to others when it's ours. The Bible teaches that we are to take leadership in our businesses, churches, communities, and especially our closest relationships—with wives, girlfriends, children. We are called to be leaders even if we, like the sitcom guy, mess up.

The problem is that most of us don't have a clue how to do it. Or we don't have the courage to go forward if we know what needs to be done. We've got our eyes focused on the wrong places. Or we're hoping for an easier solution. Maybe if we just lie down on the couch and close our eyes, the problem will take care of itself, we think.

> We are called to be leaders.... The problem is that most of us don't have a clue how to do it.

But that's not it. A big part of the solution involves keeping our eyes focused on Christ and on God's Word. Redefining winning God's way means we trust and serve God at all times. So how do we do that? What do we do? How do we "access our inner man" and move forward in maturity, with courage and wisdom, for the sake of the people who are closest to us?

THOSE EXACT TIMES

I (Colt) know what it's like to lead—and also to struggle in leadership. As a quarterback, I strive to lead my team both on and off the field. I have no problem doing that. But since I'm newly married, I'm still learning my responsibilities there. That's a fact, men: it can be harder to lead a marriage than an NFL team.

Last year Matt and Jennifer flew out to Cleveland to visit my wife and me. I was going through a rough patch in my job. As a football team, we were playing well, but we were still losing. Matt and Jenn came to a game where we were playing the Rams. In the last few minutes of the game, our team drove the ball all the way down field. Our team was in a position to win. All we needed was one field goal, and the game was ours. But because of a rare misplaced snap, our kicker missed the field goal and we lost. Man, that stunk.

That night, after the game, we were talking together as couples, and I was feeling pretty low. I was asking if it all was worth it—the punishment and pain and scrutiny of being in the spotlight all the time. Rachel confessed to Matt and Jenn how hard it was to see me depressed like that. It's not easy for a young wife to see her husband so down, and this wasn't the first time I'd been this way. It was difficult on our marriage, the stress was taking a toll, and we were finding it difficult to connect with each other in the midst of it all.

Those difficult times are when a man needs to lead.

Those exact times.

Fast-forward a year. Matt and Jenn came back to visit us again this past summer. I'd done some serious thinking and praying since the last time they'd seen us. Difficulties with my job still persisted, and the Browns had even drafted another quarterback by then. I was working hard to keep my job as a starter and, simply due to the hours I was putting in, I wasn't communicating well with the people I loved.

Matt and Jenn told us how worried they were about us. One evening during their visit, I was still at the training facility, but they were back at the apartment with my wife. Jenn asked her, "How is Colt doing? And be honest."

She said, "You know, honestly, it's been great. Colt's been a different man this year compared to what was happening inside him last year. His job is still incredibly stressful, but he's changing as a man and a husband. Now he comes home and makes a conscious effort to be present. The only thing I can figure out is that God's done a good work in his heart."

Matt and Jenn told me that was a great thing for them to hear. God has been working on my heart. I was "accessing my inner man," which means that as I continually committed my ways to the Lord, He was showing me how to truly live—not as an immature "guy" but as a mature man. Even when my job was still difficult, things at home were steadier and more stable. That's not due to anything special in me. It's all thanks to the work of God in my life.

SNAKE? *BAM!*

If you're a man and you claim the name of Christ, then you're not exempt from the role of biblical leadership. This means you do what's right and true and honorable and needs to be done, no matter how difficult a season of life you're going through. There's no such thing as a man who is a believer getting to sit on the sidelines of life and not fulfill this calling to lead.

The problem is that men are dropping the ball on this stuff. We're not doing very well at fulfilling the role of biblical manhood and leadership. As a matter of fact, when you look at the majority of—perhaps even *all*—the ills of society and the dysfunctions that plague our culture and trace them back, you will find at the bottom a man who either doesn't know how to or refuses to lead.

That might sound like a stretch. But think about this. The Bible clearly says that man has been created by God to lead in the marriage, the family, and the church. If those three things are failing, whose responsibility is it when they're falling apart? If God has called men to lead, and those things aren't working properly, then we need to take a long, hard look at the man in the mirror.

Let's take a little biblical quiz here. Who was the first person who sinned?

Eve, right? Correct. Everything was going great in the Garden of Eden, but then Eve grabbed the fruit and ate it.

Here's another question, a harder one—and this question gets to the heart of the matter for us as men even today. Who did God hold responsible for that sin?

Adam.

Why? Because God had created Adam first, and God had placed a calling on Adam to lead spiritually. God wanted Adam to be wise, man up, and be a leader. When Eve was sinning, Adam was also to blame.

Genesis 3:6 lays out the story in more depth.

> When the woman saw that the tree was good for food, and that it was a
> delight to the eyes, and that the tree was desirable to make one wise, she
> took from its fruit and ate; and she gave also to her husband with her,
> and he ate. (NASB)

So where was Adam when Eve was eating the forbidden fruit? Did you catch it in that verse? He was "with her." Adam, the world's first knucklehead, was standing there watching the whole thing go down.

You would think it would have dawned on Adam. *Oh! My wife is talking to a snake. That's not normal. The snake is telling my wife to do something the Lord has told us not to do. That's not good.* But no, he just stood by and let it all go down.

A man needs to act.

A man needs to lead.

But Adam just stood there with his hands in his pockets. (Metaphorically, of course. He didn't have pants.) He did nothing while Eve ate the fruit, and when she passed it to him, he didn't object but rather took a big bite of it himself. Adam chose the passive, immature way—and his decision affected mankind in innumerable harmful ways.

More appropriately, he should have walked into the situation and said something to his wife like "Stop! Stop! Put that fruit down!"

> Oh! My wife is talking to a snake. That's not normal.

When she suggested that he have some of the fruit himself, he could have said, "You know, darling, you're the most important thing that's ever happened to me, and I love you more than life itself. But what you're asking me to do here is something the Lord has said for us not to do, and I'm sorry, I love you, but I'm just not going to do it." Then he could have picked up a stick and beat the snake.

In other words, Adam should have stepped into that situation in the moment of his wife's greatest temptation. He should have led with maturity, wisdom, and courage. But he didn't. He didn't even open his mouth. We don't know why. Maybe he was lazy or a coward or afraid to stand up to his wife, or maybe it was because that fruit looked good to him. Whatever the reason, God had called this man to step into the situation and pursue his wife's spiritual health. But in that moment when she needed him the most, Adam did nothing. And it all fell apart.

As the rest of the story goes, God stepped into the situation and called Adam and Eve to account for their sins. But notice that God didn't call for Eve first, even though she sinned first.

> The LORD God called to the man, and said to him, "Where are you?"
> (Genesis 3:9, NASB)

Now, it's important to understand that when God said to Adam, "Where are you?" it doesn't mean that God couldn't find him. God is omniscient. He knows everything all the time. So it's more like God had cleared His throat and in a deep voice was saying, *"Boy, where you at?"* God was calling Adam to account for his sin.

This theme is fleshed out in Romans 5:12–14. Paul talks about the exact moment when Adam and Eve sinned. That original sin was imparted to all mankind because of the first humans' sin.

> Just as sin came into the world through one man, and death through
> sin, and so death spread to all men because all sinned—for sin

indeed was in the world before the law was given, but sin is not counted where there is no law. Yet death reigned from Adam to Moses. (ESV)

Scripture is clear. The sin of all mankind can be traced back to *one man* who sat on the sidelines. Adam was either too afraid or had absolutely no clue how to lead. He didn't know how to fulfill the role God had placed in His life. And it changed everything for the worse.

LEADERSHIP SINS

The lack-of-leadership plague has spread throughout the male population ever since Adam. We're not in the Garden of Eden anymore, standing by the tree of knowledge with some tasty-looking but forbidden fruit in our hands. Yet we come to plenty other points of decision where we have to choose whether to step up and lead as God wants us to or drop the ball and do nothing—or maybe worse than nothing.

Let's put a name on it when we choose a course of action that's different from biblical leadership. It's *sin.* In fact, a whole series of sins tend to characterize men who are failing in masculine leadership.

Take some time to carefully examine your life. Do you recognize any of the following sins as holding you back from being the leader God has called you to be? They all represent different ways of shirking on your duty to lead.[2]

1. The sin of acting macho

Being macho is a pretentious, swaggering display of false masculinity. It's the idea that whatever women do, you do the opposite. Such as, since women are nurturing, you're not. Or since women are caring, you're not.

If you're macho, then (assuming you have kids) you're the guy who never changes a diaper. If your eight-year-old daughter asks you to read her a book about princesses, you say no way. You're the guy yelling loudest on your son's baseball team—but not in a good way, cheering him on. You're yelling at him to win at all costs. Or you're yelling at the ump to stop being such a jerk, even to the point where you've become a spectacle. A sports dad of the worst kind.

> Being macho is...the idea that whatever women do, you do the opposite.

If you've succumbed to the sin of acting macho, then you're the guy who, even though the Scriptures say hospitality is a spiritual gift of both women *and* men, would never think to help your wife tidy up the house if company is coming over. That's what women do, you say. But a man who leads biblically values hospitality because God values it. If company is coming over, a true man of God knows that part of his call is to make sure his house is in order. That means either helping his wife out or doing the job himself.

Instead of being macho, which is really an abdication of leadership, Philippians 4:5 points to true biblical leadership: "Let your gentleness be evident to all" (NIV). *Gentleness* means you're not severe or rough. A man of gentleness is the coolest guy in the room, a man of peace, even in the face of the most ruthless attack. Want to access your inner man? Don't swagger. Don't put on some kind of ridiculous show of masculinity. Be a true gentleman.

2. The sin of materialism

Many men think that their biggest calling is providing for their family. From there, they reason that making money is the best—or even the only—thing a man should do.

Wrong.

It's true that a part of a man's calling is to provide for his family. It's his job to wake up to the alarm in the morning, crawl out of bed, go to work, and make sure his family's needs are met. But too many men think their job is to buy everything their kids want, like that new Xbox or trip to Disneyland. Or to make sure that their wife drives the latest and greatest SUV. Or that their family lives in the best house they can possibly afford.

Instead, what children and spouses really want from men is more of *them*. What your wife really wants is a husband who pursues her and cherishes her and cares about her emotional and spiritual needs. What your children really want is to spend more time with you.

Our call to provide exists, yes, but that's certainly not where the calling ends. Want to access your inner man? Watch out for the lure of materialism. Learn to seek after what's truly important in life instead.

3. The sin of anger

Anger can sometimes be warranted. But anger becomes a sin when you become the guy who leads with your temper instead of your tenderness.

Guys like this need to win every debate with their wife or kids or neighbor or coworker or the driver on the freeway next to them. These men have forgotten that Jesus displays tremendous kindness, even to the point of using kindness as a tool to bring people to repentance (Romans 2:4).

A kind man is a man who reflects the characteristics of Jesus. If someone has wronged you, kindness will lead him or her to change, not wrath. Want to be the man you are called to be? Don't be the guy who yells at everyone. Be a man who leads with thoughtfulness, reasonableness, and good temper instead.

4. The sins of dominance and control

Sometimes men don't realize how strong an influence they have over the people around them—the people closest in their lives. Dominance can become a sin when your attitude becomes "It's either my way or the highway."

A man who controls his spouse leaves no room for her input and wisdom to help direct the family's decisions. A controlling man is an exasperating man. He's not flexible, even when it's most prudent. This guy's home is a place of constant correction and critique instead of loving, gentle admonition. He leads out of guilt and condemnation.

By contrast, 1 Corinthians 13 describes a love that keeps no record of evil and hardly notices when others do things wrong. That's the type of man we're called to be—go there when you want to access your inner man.

5. The sins of laziness and immaturity

A man who struggles with laziness and immaturity has never grown up. This man's maturity level is stuck in a state of perpetual adolescence. He might dominate on the latest Xbox game and fantasy football, but he has no clue how to keep his hands off his girlfriend and lead her in purity. He might dream of a high-paying job, but his work ethic demonstrates unresponsiveness and a lack of teachability. He might think his needs aren't being met at church, but his walk with Christ is much more likely to be spurred on by the latest podcast. Instead of being the guy who's on his face before the Lord, studying Scripture intently and listening to the voice of the Holy Spirit for direction, he's the guy who quits when situations start to get tough.

This man is a man in body alone. The rest of him is stuck in immaturity.

His mind is not matured to a point where he consistently walks in wisdom.

His mouth has not matured so that he's speaking words that build up, nurture, and help others out (James 3:1–12).

His soul has not grown up in Christ to where he wants spiritual meat, not spiritual milk (Hebrews 5:12).

That's what needs to change. It's time to step away from the sin of perpetual adolescence and grow up.

6. The sins of emotional and spiritual absence

This is the guy who's dependable. He's a good guy. He's not going to cheat on his wife or beat her or leave her destitute. But his wife cannot remember the last time he took her face in his hands and told her, "You are the most amazing woman I have ever known." He's physically present, but he's emotionally not there.

This is the dad whose kids don't know what it's like to crawl up in his lap and fall asleep, or to roll around on the ground with him and act crazy and be chased and tickled. This dad's kids don't know what it's like to have their father tuck them in at night and have him pray for them and read Scripture, because he's got some important television shows he needs to watch. This guy's wife doesn't know what it's like to be spiritually led by her husband. He's expecting his pastor to do it. So he never reads the Bible with her or prays with her or talks about spiritual matters or sets an example of spiritual maturity for her.

This man needs to invest himself fully in his true calling. That means in all areas of his life—physically, spiritually, mentally, and emotionally. Want to access your inner man? Be there. Be all there.

7. The sins of spiritual legalism and hyperspirituality

This man doesn't feel real to the people around him because he's afraid to admit how much he needs the gospel of Jesus Christ. He's the guy who has all the right answers even though he's really struggling inside. He's afraid to raise his hand and say to a close group of spiritually minded men, "This is where I sin, and this is where I deeply need Jesus."

With men who have the sin of spiritual legalism, God is often doing some good stuff in their hearts. He's changing them and messing them up in really good ways. But instead of the hand of God emerging in their lives in the form of humility, the influence falsely emerges in arrogance. These guys critique everything but lead absolutely nothing. They're the armchair quarterbacks of the worst kind.

Following Jesus isn't about legalism or rule following. Want to access your inner man? Psalm 119:32 says, "I run in the path of your commands, for you have set my heart free" (NIV). That freedom is a key characteristic of a life of following Jesus. It's not the freedom to do anything you like anytime you like. It's the freedom of a yoke that's easy and a burden that's light (Matthew 11:30).

8. The sins of hedonism and frivolity

This is the guy who's spending his time playing games, going out partying, and generally just wasting his life.

People often love this guy, but nobody is being led by this guy because he's not doing anything that matters. This guy's goals are more likely to be centered on his golf handicap and his stock portfolio than on the spiritual environment he helps create in his home and in his wife's or his children's walks with the Lord. He's more likely to be found playing poker with the boys than pursuing and cherishing the heart of his wife. He spends more time surfing the web than he does serving his church. This is the guy who trades the eternal and the significant for the temporary and the fun.

Want to access your inner man? Sure, there's a time and a place for joy, pleasure, and true leisure in the life of a man. But there's also a huge place for serious-mindedness, hard work, and fulfilling your responsibilities.

It's Not About Being Perfect

It can be easy for men to read through a list like the one above and be tempted to walk out the side door. We both admit that we've struggled with sins like these as much as the next man. So how do any of us begin to tackle the sins on this list?

> The real power to change always comes from Jesus working inside us.

The answer isn't about trying harder. Plenty of men do that, and it just doesn't work. Sure, willpower factors into the equation. We can decide to be leaders, and we have the power to choose whether or not we will stay stuck in passivity. But the real power to change always comes from Jesus working inside us.

A good place to begin is to walk through that list with someone else. If you're married or dating, work through this list with your spouse or significant other. Let the woman in your life say things like, "Yeah, I see this in your life" or "Actually, you're doing really well in this area." Don't be defensive when she answers you honestly; just repent, if necessary, and ask God for the power to go forward. Another great place to work through this list is with a group of godly men in your church or spiritual assembly. Work through this list as iron sharpens iron, and let others hold you accountable as you, in turn, speak into their lives.

It's so important to close this chapter with this truth in our minds—we all fall short of the glory of God. That's where grace enters in. There has been only one perfect man who has ever lived, and His name is Jesus Christ. Romans 5:17 tells us that even though sin entered the world through one man, Adam, the restoring work of Jesus Christ trumps all that Adam ever did. That verse says, "If, because of one man's trespass, death reigned through that one man, much more will those who receive the abundance of grace and the free gift of righteousness…" *Stop right there!* Who's received an abundance of grace and the free gift of righteousness? That's us. Okay, we can proceed to complete the verse: "Much more will those who receive the abundance of grace and the free gift of righteousness reign in life through the one man Jesus Christ" (ESV).

Jesus is the only man who has ever lived life perfectly. Trusting in Him is the only hope we have. He's the only man who lived a perfect life. He died on the cross, was raised in power, and now lives in us and gives us the ability to walk boldly throughout life and look more and more like Him as we live our lives.

Our prayer is that you would trust Jesus to continue to do a good work in you. The invitation is not to lower the bar. It's about raising the bar in the hearts and lives of men everywhere. It's time we all started living up to the calling God has placed on our lives as men.

We can do this, all of us, together.

In the next two chapters we'll look at some of the most important ways a man is a leader. Are you taking the initiative with your wife and giving her what she needs—your love? Are you providing spiritual leadership in your home for your wife and children?

Love Her First

A husband takes the lead in his marriage
by giving his wife the love she craves.

Husbands, love your wives.

—Ephesians 5:25, ESV

I (Colt) have been married since 2010, and I love my wife more than you can imagine. I'd say we're at a really good place in our marriage these days, but it hasn't always been this way. Honestly, there have been some times when I've just plain blown it as a husband.

The rocky times we've had so far have all sprung from me and my heavy work schedule. Frankly, it's been hard for me to love my wife as Christ loved the church and to serve her first when my world revolves around football and all the hours I spend out on the field. When I first got married, I knew in my head that the most important thing was loving and serving my wife every day. But to be honest, I didn't do it the way I needed to.

One example of this was in the area of prayer. Now, I pray a lot. I pray before I go to bed, pray at meals, pray in my times with the Lord, and even pray at times during games. But for some reason, early on in my marriage, I struggled to pray with my wife. I had read and heard in sermons over the years that praying as a married couple was essential, but when we sat down together to eat or lay down together at night, I knew I should pray, but I just couldn't seem to do it. My wife even asked me about it, and I changed the subject. I knew what I needed to do, but I lacked the courage and the know-how to do it.

I think most men can point to a similar struggle. When it comes to marriage, we need a little "how to" instruction, even if we only admit it among ourselves. It's not that marriage is a huge burden or that our wives are un-lovable. It's just that we need guidance on how to best love our wives and on what ways of loving will meet the scriptural principles God gave us and will be interpreted by our wives as love.

> In our marriages we lead by taking the initiative to give our wife what she needs most—our love.

We've already seen how, as men, we're supposed to be leaders. In our marriages we lead by taking the initiative to give our wife what she needs most—our love. And that's so even if she isn't giving us everything we'd like. Over and over again, I've seen how a man's taking leadership by loving his wife *first* leads her to eventually reciprocate by giving him the respect he craves. So I hold that out as a strong hope to you if you're unsatisfied in your marriage. But whatever your wife's response may be, your responsibility is to be faithful to God's call upon you in this area and to lead with love—that's the real win when it comes to marriage. And that's what we're getting into in this chapter.

If you're single, take notes—there's plenty of good stuff here for you too.

THAT FEELING OF DISTANCE

I (Matt) have been married for sixteen years now, and I was a miserable failure as a husband for the first ten. And the thing is, when it was happening, I never even knew it.

During those first ten years, Jennifer and I almost never argued. She is really laid back and not a complainer. On top of that, she has a really strong walk with Jesus Christ. So in many ways she was doing fine without me leading her or engaging with her as I should have. Meanwhile, I was busy and happy and thought everything was all right. To be honest, my marriage was so smooth that I patted myself on the back, thinking, *I'm a rock-star husband. I have this thing down. Man, just look at me.*

Then something happened that I'll never forget. One day my wife sat me down and started crying. "Matt," she said, "I want you to understand that I would never leave you or cheat on you. But our marriage is just not working out."

I was shocked. "What do you mean, Jenn? What's going on?"

"You're here, Matt, but you're just not *here.* We're distant and I never feel connected to you. When we were dating, you totally pursued me. But when we got married, you stopped pursuing me. You pursue the church. You pursue your work. But you don't pursue *me.*" Then she added one phrase that really hit me: "We're just so distant."

I asked for an example. Jenn got quiet, then told me a story.

One Sunday she was coming out of church. It had been a full morning already, and she had our three young children with her and was carrying a stroller, a diaper bag, and all the stuff young moms need to cart around when they have little kids. As usual, I was off somewhere, busy with church stuff. A well-meaning man saw that she was struggling and offered to help. He opened her car door and helped corral our kids into the backseat. Basically, he did everything a good husband would have done. Nothing more happened. The guy said, "Have a good day," and walked away.

"I'd never, ever cheat on you," she repeated when she was telling me the story, "but I want you to know how good it felt for a man to pay attention to me...just for once."

That statement right there made me realize the depths of how poor a husband I'd been. I'd been so neglecting my wife emotionally that the simple act of a guy opening a door for my wife could fill a huge empty place in her heart.

That conversation woke me up in a big way, and I realized there's a lot more to being a good husband than I had dreamed.

Safe to say, a lot of men and women struggle in their marriages. I used to do a lot of marriage counseling at the church. Right about the time Jenn had this talk with me, I was counseling four couples where, in three of the four situations, the wife was having an affair. During the counseling sessions, all three wives separately articulated the same thing. They pointed at their husbands and said, "I really love my husband, and he's the one I truly want to be with... but he's just so distant."

I'd heard my wife say the same word—*distant*. And that sent a chill through me.

In the counseling cases, the next statement out of all three women's mouths was equally similar. The specific scenarios were different, but all three women talked about how some other guy wasn't being distant. "But there was this guy at work who wasn't distant. This guy at work pursued me. He cherished me. My husband didn't."

I remember sitting there as the guy doing the counseling and thinking, *What's the deal with this need of women to be cherished and pursued?* I still had no idea.

A Book You Don't Need to Read

About that same time, a book began to get really popular. It was called *Twilight*, and every woman I knew was reading this book. I didn't want to read it, so I bought the book, handed it to my wife, and said, "Babe, would you read this, please? Figure out what's going on." Jenn is not a huge reader. And this book is thick. But she picked it up and read it straight through in two days. When I asked her about it, she explained that the book was about a teenage vampire who falls in love with a nonvampire girl.

One afternoon I walked into the office at church, and six of our staff women were talking about the book over lunch. I approached them and said,

"I keep hearing about this *Twilight* book. Why is every woman in the world reading it?" They answered, "Edward Cullen is the main character of the book. He is the perfect man."

"The perfect man?" I asked. "He's an albino vampire!"

They laughed and explained to me that Edward falls in love with a human girl named Bella. She's sort of an ordinary girl, but Edward falls for her and begins to pursue her in a highly romantic, nonvampire sort of way. The women in my office said things like, "He's just so *into* her. He cherishes her."

> "The perfect man?" I asked. "He's an albino vampire!"

They explained to me that *Twilight* provides a picture of what every woman wants in a relationship, minus the vampire part.

Finally I started putting two and two together.

I had a wife who was saying, "You're not pursuing me and cherishing me."

I encountered women in my church who were having affairs because their husbands were not pursuing and cherishing them.

I had every woman in my church reading a book about a pasty vampire because he pursued and cherished the girl.

Now, if you are a woman and you are reading this book, I want to say one thing, just in case it needs saying. Edward Cullen does not exist in real life. *Twilight* is chick porn. The book offers a false fantasy. That's all it is. There is only one man who can love you and pursue you and cherish you perfectly, and it's not Edward Cullen. It's not even your husband. It's Jesus.

Having got that off my chest, I think all the attention given the *Twilight* books teaches us something. *Twilight* is a testament to the failure of the American marriage and men's inability to understand and meet the deep needs of a woman's heart.

Know this: There is a deep need in the soul of every woman—whether it's your girlfriend, fiancée, wife, or daughter—to be cherished and pursued and loved and pointed to Jesus by the man God has placed in her life.

If your significant other doesn't get that deep need met from you, she'll be reading *Twilight,* or something like that.

Or she'll sit you down and say you're not connecting anymore.

Or, like the women I counseled, she'll have an affair.

What the Bible Says

The good news is that the Bible gives us men clear advice about how to love our wives. The real win means trusting the Lord and walking with Jesus and living your life the way God defined it.

Ephesians 5:23–24 says, "The husband is the head of the wife even as Christ is the head of the church, his body, and is himself its Savior. Now as the church submits to Christ, so also wives should submit in everything to their husbands" (ESV).

Verse 25 gives men the direct command:

Husbands, love your wives, as Christ loved the church and gave himself
up for her.

That's the command. It's short, straightforward, and easy to remember— *Husbands, love.* It's an active command. You don't love your wife by doing *nothing.*

Which begs the question: If you're going to love your wife as Christ loved the church, how do you do that?

Well, Christ loved the church in thousands of ways. He died for the church, to begin with. Another big way Christ loved the church is that He *loved her first.* That may sound insignificant, but the point is that He initiated the love. First John 4:19 says, "We love because *he first loved us*" (ESV). Meaning Jesus didn't sit back with His arms folded and expect us to approach Him and love Him and serve Him first, and then maybe He would love us back. In spite of our dysfunctions, shortcomings, failures, and sins, He initiated the love. He loved us first. He loved us anyway. That's leadership. Are you doing the same with your wife?

Think of how powerful the example of Jesus is. I (Matt) had been a Christian my whole life, but I'd fallen away from Jesus my first year at Texas A&M. As a freshman, I wasn't doing well at all. I was mired in all the regular sexual sins that young single guys are prone to. I was desperately lonely and had no purpose in my life. All the stuff I thought was going to make me happy wasn't doing its job. There was absolutely nothing of merit in my life where God could have looked at me and said, "That's the guy I want to go love."

At that point, what Christ could have done is what a lot of American husbands do. He could have stood on the sidelines and said, "Hey, Matt, if you want to get something out of this relationship, then you need to come and love Me. You need to get your act together and come serve Me. Then maybe I'll love you back."

That's not what He did at all. When nothing in my life warranted His favor, Christ loved me first. He filled the void of loneliness in my life. He became my constant companion, the greatest friend in my life. He forgave me of my sin, made me clean, and invited me into the greatest adventure I could ever imagine. I still am standing in His perfect plan for my life today. He came to me and He loved me, and He loved me first.

For the first ten years I was married to Jennifer, my attitude was not one where I loved her first. My attitude was more like, "Jenn, you need to respect me. Jenn, you need to honor me. Jenn, you need to take care of my needs. If you act right, the way I want you to act, then I'll pursue you and cherish you and love you." I think that's how a lot of men treat their wives.

But Jesus modeled the exact opposite. When we'd done nothing right—in fact, when we had done everything wrong, He came and He loved us. He loved us first.

Men, this is the calling of your life. Husbands, love your wives as Christ Jesus loved the church. That means it doesn't matter what your wife is doing or not doing. You take the initiative, and you love her.

How to Love Your Wife

So, what might that love look like?

It begins by finding out the best ways that she receives love. Then you go to her and love her that way.

You may have heard about a book called *The Five Love Languages* by Dr. Gary Chapman.[1] Its premise is that everybody on the planet receives love in at least one of five different ways.

- *By acts of service.* This is when you say, "Let me do that for you." It might be vacuuming the stairs or doing the dishes.
- *By gifts being given.* This is where thoughtful gestures demonstrate love. You bring your wife a bouquet of flowers after work. You buy her perfume or clothes.
- *By physical touch.* This is where hugs, holding hands, and other forms of physical affection demonstrate love.
- *By receiving words of affirmation.* This is where hearing words means a lot to your spouse, such as "I really care for you," and "I love you," and "You're doing a great job."
- *By spending quality time with that person.* This is where full, undivided attention speaks volumes.

Men, here's what it looks like to love your wife. Find the way your wife receives love, and then love her that way. That way you'll know that your message of love will get through to her.

The problem is, many men reverse the order. They think about how they like to receive love, and they assume it's the same as their wife's love language. So they show her love the way *they* like to receive it, not the way *she* does.

That's what I was doing wrong at first. I loved my wife, but I didn't show her love the way she best received it. For instance, one time I bought her a pearl necklace. She liked it, appreciated it, and wore it, but it didn't really minister to her. It didn't really communicate love to her like I had hoped it would. She didn't *feel* deeply loved as I'd hoped she would.

I have a friend whose wife's love language centers around acts of service, which I desperately wish was my wife's love language. All he does after dinner is do the dishes, and it's guaranteed sex. I mean *guaranteed*, every time. When I heard about that, I immediately started thinking, *Yeah, I can do that.* So Jenn cooks dinner. We eat. I get up and do the dishes. Then she walks up to me,

> Find the way your wife receives love, and then love her that way.

pats me on the shoulder, says, "Thanks for doing the dishes," and walks off. I'm like, *What? That's it?* She appreciated my act of service, but that's not really what meets the deep needs of her soul.

It took me awhile to learn what makes her feel most cherished and valued. Expressing love isn't about following a formula, but I discovered one thing that really speaks to her: writing her a note. And when I write a note, I tell her how much she means to me. If I really take the time and the note is handwritten (not an e-mail), that ministers to her in ways nothing else will. I found out recently that she's kept every note I have ever written to her our entire marriage. From me, my wife would rather have a handwritten note than a diamond necklace.

That's the point—find out how your wife or girlfriend best receives love. Not what you love to receive or love to do for her, but what *she* loves. It won't necessarily be the same for your wife as it is for mine, but that's part of the joy you experience in the continual pursuit of your wife.

Another big area where I can show love to my wife is by spending quality time with her. Good things happen if I help her get the kids to bed, then turn the television off, get her a cup of coffee, sit down, and talk, just asking her things like "How was your day? How are you and the kids doing? How was your time with Jesus today? How's your walk? How's your prayer life?" It deeply affects her heart and ministers to her. She will walk away from a fifteen-minute conversation with me, one where I'm actually there and paying attention to her, and say in her heart, *Wow, my husband cherishes me and pursues me.*

Now this isn't always easy. Absolutely not. Honestly, I don't like writing notes. And I hate talking. I talk for a living. The last thing I feel like doing after a day at work is talking more.

But I love my wife.

And the last time I checked, the calling on my life as the husband of Jennifer Carter is to love her as Christ loved the church, which means I need to go to her and love her first in the way she needs to be loved.

GIVING YOURSELF UP

Love doesn't stop there. The process actually gets more difficult for us men. Ephesians 5:25 says, "Husbands, love your wives, as Christ loved the church *and gave himself up for her*" (ESV).

Jesus, as the head of the church, could have exercised His authority in any way He wanted. But how did He lead the church? He gave Himself up for her. In Jesus's case, He laid His life down.

Now I've never personally been put in a place where I needed to actually die for my wife. But there are a lot of other ways that I can give myself up for her.

One is the area of personal purity. I love Jesus and I'm called to personal purity because of that. I'm also committed to personal purity because I want my wife to know she's the only woman in my life. More than mere knowledge, I want her to feel and experience that commitment.

Here are some of the things I do: I don't ever travel alone. When I speak at conferences, I have a male colleague come with me. I will never be alone the entire conference. I will never be alone in my hotel room. I have protective software on my computer and phone. I don't want to have access to the Internet when somebody is not watching. I want my wife to know that my eyes belong to Jesus and they belong to her.

At home, I have a password on my television that blocks harmful content. My wife has the password. She has access to my e-mail, phone, and Twitter account. My life is an open book because I am called to love my wife the way Christ Jesus loved the church by giving Himself up for her. I purposely choose to have the same bedtime as her because I don't want to be up by myself in the house all alone. That's when the temptation comes to do crazy stuff. By not staying up later, I can't watch all the programs I'm inclined to watch, but I do that because I want to give myself up because Jesus gave Himself up for us. You might think my actions are a bit excessive. But I am weary of watching men flush their lives and families down the toilet because of affairs. Maybe it's time we got a little excessive in the arena of purity.

Another way I give myself up for her is in the area of conflict. This, too, is a Christlike way to behave. First Peter 2:23 says, "When he [Jesus] was reviled, he did not revile in return; when he suffered, he did not threaten, but continued entrusting himself to him who judges justly" (ESV).

If I disagree with my wife about something, I always face the temptation to "win"—whatever we're disagreeing about. But where does that get me, and where does it get her? When we get into a disagreement, we can talk things through, sure. But my aim is to love my wife, not to win an argument. A big part of that means I just need to learn when to keep my mouth shut.

AT THE END OF THE DAY

I've had some similar struggles in my (Colt's) marriage. A quarterback is under a lot of pressure during the season. I live in a glass box where the media know exactly what I'm doing. I'm the leader of my team, and every day I spend a lot of time trying to perfect what I do. Plus, the work environment itself isn't easy—just as I bet it isn't easy for your job. Each day I'm in an environment

> I live in a glass box where the media know exactly what I'm doing.

where I'm driven to succeed no matter what. I'm pretty much still the youngest guy in my locker room. So when I go home, it takes me awhile to get out of work mode—you know, that feeling of being so focused on work I can't leave it behind.

All that first year after my wife and I were married, I'd come home and sit on the couch, expecting some alone time like I had before I was married. I needed some space to breathe and relax. For the first thirty or forty minutes after walking through the front door, I hardly engaged with my wife at all. I'd come home expecting to be served dinner. After dinner, I'd sit on the couch again and maybe watch a TV show or some of the film I didn't get a chance to see during the day, and then go to bed.

My wife was too kind to me and didn't confront me about my behavior. But I could sense something was wrong. Finally I got to the point of being convicted about how I was acting toward her. One day she came to me, as sweet as she is and as nice as she is, and admitted she couldn't take it anymore. She shared her feelings, saying I wasn't living up to the expectations she had for me as a husband. "With the amount of time you spend on football, it's like I don't even have a husband," she said. That hurt.

So with God's help, I've begun to get wiser in my marriage. Playing football has not gotten any easier. In fact, in some ways I'm going through a harder season now than I ever have before. I probably spend more time at work today than ever. But there's been a shift. Now when I come home, I purposely choose to love my wife the way I need to and express that love. I've learned a lot about how to engage with my wife.

One of her love languages is time spent together. So today I make a greater effort to spend time with her and talk with her. I ask, "How are you doing? How was your day? What went on today? Who have you talked to? How's your family? How's my family? How's your walk with Jesus?" Our time together now is much more meaningful.

Recently a Navy SEAL came to our training facility in Cleveland to talk with us. One of the guys in the locker room asked, "What's the most important thing you do in the SEALs that involves your family?"

The SEAL said, "I leave my work at work. When I'm home, I'm engaged with my family. There's a small amount of time when I get to be with my family, and that small time is all I've got. So I encourage you guys—you work hard, you compete, you do everything you can to be as successful as you can. But when you go home, you leave your work at work. When you go home, engage with your wife, talk with your kids, raise your family, and be the leader of your household."

It was late in my rookie year when I heard that, and I realized that I was approaching my relationship with my wife the wrong way. Since then I've changed the way I treat my wife. The amount of meaningful time we spend together has gone up, and it's made a world of difference in our relationship.

Our marriage is strong today. I'm not saying it's always easy, but that's the way it needs to be done.

A Love That Works Well

Now, both of us (Colt and Matt) realize there are allowances. It's okay for a man to want to decompress at the end of a day. Work does require an awful lot for a man, and it's difficult to be totally at work, then flip a switch and be totally at home.

When my wife and I (Colt) figured this out, we prayed about it, talked about it, and I realized I needed to change the way I loved and served my wife. She said, "Colt, I truly know that this is a hard thing for you to do. You're consumed by your work and the pressures of your work. Just take a few minutes when you get home to decompress."

So that's what I do now. I go into my room, maybe look at a newspaper or magazine or just sit on the couch and take a fifteen-minute nap. That gives me time to take a deep breath, flip the switch, and make the transition. But when those fifteen minutes are over, I've prepared myself to come in and be a husband. My wife is not at all high maintenance. But you can't imagine how much our relationship changed for the better when we both made those little adjustments. We're doing great.

I (Matt) do a similar thing. It used to be that when I came home, Jenn gave me thirty minutes to myself. That changed when we had kids. Jenn is a stay-at-home mom, so she has the kids from the time I leave in the morning until the time I get home at night. She's hard at it all day long, changing diapers, cooking, cleaning, and feeding kids. So these days I come home and give her a thirty- to forty-five-minute break. I take the kids and let her get some decompression time. And then we start engaging as a family.

> There's a bridge I cross over on the drive home,...when I get to that bridge, I shift my mind-set from pastor of Austin Stone to pastor of... Jennifer, Annie, J. D., and Sammy Carter.

It's difficult, because like Colt, I want that down time after work too. So one solution we've worked out is that I purposely and strategically decompress in the car on the way home. That's when I consciously let go of the stuff at the office. There's a bridge I cross over on the drive home, and I made a commitment that when I get to that bridge, I shift my mind-set from pastor of Austin Stone to pastor of my family: Jennifer, Annie, J. D., and Sammy Carter. When I walk in the front door, I can start serving them.

As Christ Loved the Church

Men, what are you called to do?

You're called to love your wife as Christ loved the church.

You give yourself up. You love. That's what redefining success looks like, even if your wife is falsely accusing you; or if she does not understand your heart; or if she is being contentious, combative, or insulting; or if she is not respecting you, serving you, or taking care of your needs. It doesn't matter. You love her first. You give yourself up for her. That's what it means to lead your wife in love.

Now does that mean you never speak truth to your wife? No. Does that mean that you never gently admonish her and lead her in the way of truth? No, there are going to be times when you need to do that, when you need to speak truth to your wife.

But what it means is that, in conflict, you take the initiative to bring peace. That's hard, especially when you think you're right. But you take the initiative to bring peace because that's what Jesus Christ did and calls us to do too.

When the volume of voices and the harshness of words begin to escalate, you take the initiative to de-escalate. It's the way that men can properly show their strength—not by giving a punch, even a figurative punch, but by taking punches over and over again and loving in return. And when you do that, you look a whole lot like Jesus Christ.

One of my all-time favorite authors is John Piper. He talks about how women, particularly wives, can be prone to doubt themselves. They wonder if they're what their husbands wanted. They wonder if they please their husbands.

I get that. That's why wise husbands spend the rest of their lives answering that question. Men, we need to continually tell our wives, "Babe, I'd marry you all over again. You're cherished. I want you."

That's what we're talking about.

Husband, love your wife. Love her first.

When we as men take the lead and radically love our wives, we can have absolute confidence that we're doing what God invites us to do. The benefit is ours as well as our family's. And this brings us to another aspect of male leadership—leading our wives and kids in spiritual things. Did you know that you're the pastor for your home? It's true. And you don't need to be intimidated by that.

Keep going. There's more good stuff ahead.

Rev. You

Men have the privilege and responsibility to provide spiritual leadership in the home.

> Husbands, love your wives, as Christ loved the church and gave himself up for her, that he might sanctify her, having cleansed her by the washing of water with the word.
>
> —EPHESIANS 5:25–26, ESV

I (Colt) realized during my second season in the NFL that I had put my God-given call to lead my wife on the back burner. I was starting that year for the Cleveland Browns, so literally every waking minute of my life was being consumed with football, preparation for football, or thoughts about football. My wife's spiritual health was not something I was spending a ton of time thinking about.

After some prayer and good old-fashioned conviction by the Holy Spirit, I set about remedying this situation after the season ended. As soon as we got back home to Austin, I took the lead and started making some calls to my home church to see if there was a Bible study that Rachel and I could attend during the off-season. After some research, we found one and spent one night a week with other couples, praying and studying the Scriptures together. It meant more to my wife than you can imagine that I took the initiative to ensure that she was growing spiritually.

Men, this is our responsibility. At church we've got a pastor looking out for our family's spiritual well-being. But at home we need to make sure that our wife and kids are growing toward Christ all the time. In effect, we're the pastors at home.

Would it be easier just to let it slide? Sure. But that's a loser move.

To figure out what spiritual leadership in the home really means and how to pull it off, we're going to start by going further with a Bible passage we first focused on in the previous chapter.

Sanctifying

Honestly, there are some heavy, crazy passages in the Bible about sacrificial love. One is Ephesians 5:25–28, which we've already started looking at as it relates to our responsibility to love our wives. But there's a whole other dimension to this passage.

The Ephesians 5 passage relates specifically to married men, but its implications are far-reaching no matter what your marital status might be. At its core, the passage talks about what it looks like to love others sacrificially and be a spiritual leader in the relationships that matter most to us. Here it is:

> Husbands, love your wives, as Christ loved the church and gave himself
> up for her, that he might sanctify her, having cleansed her by the
> washing of water with the word, so that he might present the church to
> himself in splendor, without spot or wrinkle or any such thing, that she
> might be holy and without blemish. In the same way husbands should
> love their wives. (ESV)

These Scripture verses lay the groundwork for the role you can play in how God sanctifies other people, specifically your wife.

To clarify, sanctification isn't the same thing as justification. That's another big word, but *justification* basically means that at the moment of your salvation God looks at you and says, "That's My son—and I see him as completely holy, like Jesus." Justification means that you're made righteous in the sight of God.

> The day you get married, you become a lead pastor.

Sanctification is something every Christ follower goes through his or her whole life. It's the process of becoming more and more like Jesus. And Scripture teaches us that when we get married, the primary person God looks at in the sanctification process of our wives is you and me—the husband in her life. It's not her pastor. It's not the guy she is listening to on a podcast. It's not Beth Moore. It's you, friend. The day you get married, you become a lead pastor, the man who disciples your wife. Your calling is to be a minister in your marriage, and you are not exempt from the role if you don't feel equipped to do it.

Most of us men grasp the first part of that passage in Ephesians—the command to love our wives. Sometimes we struggle with knowing exactly how to do it best, but the command itself is straightforward. But the second part of the passage is where things get more complex. What does it mean that Christ cleanses the church by the washing of water with the Word? And what does it mean for Christ to present the church to Himself in splendor, without spot or wrinkle or any such thing, that she might be holy and without blemish?

At first glance, the simple application is that as husbands we are to make sure that our wives are regularly reading the Bible. Sure, they have a responsibility in this area too. But it's our call to model the process and to encourage it in them.

But the passage means more than that. "Having cleansed her by the washing of water" is not talking about baptism. It refers back to a practice that happened in biblical times. Back in the day when this passage was written, the women in a bridal party would wash a bride-to-be with water before she was married. It was primarily symbolic. It meant that the bride was now ready to be presented to her groom. She was clean, pure, and spotless in his sight.

That's what the Scriptures say we husbands are responsible to do in our wives' lives. And really, it's also a call to all single men today regarding how they treat the women they date. We're not actually supposed to take our girlfriends, fiancés, or wives out to the rain barrel and dunk them in a tub. The cleansing is a symbolic action. We're called to be responsible for a woman's purity—morally, spiritually, emotionally, and mentally. Our call is to do everything we can to help her grow in the Lord.

Of course, the implication is that we're doing that sort of washing for ourselves too. We're not commanded to "wash" our wives because we men are superclean to begin with and our wives are morally dirty and need cleaning. Nothing of the sort. We as men are called to live sanctified lives first. Then instead of viewing our wives or girlfriends as people we use for our own selfish gain, we're to lead them down the same path of sanctification that we're already supposed to be traveling down.

That's your call—to actively engage in the sanctification process of your spouse, so that she will be ready to be presented to her ultimate Bridegroom, Jesus Christ. From the moment she walks down the aisle with a ring on her finger, until the moment at the end when she's buried in the ground, you are to engage in her sanctification process so that you can present her to Jesus Christ without spot or blemish.

That's a pretty tall order, because this act of cleansing involves more than symbolism. It's an overall attitude, yes, but there are specific actions we can take in the process.

As the lead pastor of your marriage, you become the spiritual leader of your marriage, so this is what you do. You begin by taking an overall active role in her spiritual life as well as your own. You ask yourself questions such as, *How's my wife's spiritual life going? Is she praying? When things go wrong, is she holding things inside worrying, or is she hitting her knees and turning to Jesus? Is she being mentored by an older, godly woman? Is she actively engaged in passing along her spiritual wisdom to those younger than her?*

You look for ways you can encourage her in her role as a worshiper and minister. Do you know what your wife's spiritual gifts are and whether she is using them? Are you challenging her to get in the fight and to use the spiritual gifts that God gave her to expand and grow and build the body of Christ?

You protect and shelter her and remove things from your culture of marriage that might hinder her growth. As a husband, do you know your wife's struggles, temptations, failures, and sins? Are you creating a grace-filled environment in your marriage, so that your wife can come to you and say, "This is where I'm failing" (and you can say the same to her)? When you confess your sins to each other, you can help speak the truth of the Word of God with love into those failures.

> Too many wives are widows *spiritually*. We're with them physically, but they are spiritually all by themselves.

You actively spend time in helping your wife grow spiritually. Are you the guy who is setting the culture of your marriage in such a way that in areas including finances, time management, gender roles, and sexuality, the Word of God is speaking more deeply into your life than the latest sitcom?

That's your calling as a husband—to be the spiritual leader of the relationship. Too many wives are widows *spiritually*. We're with them physically, but they are spiritually all by themselves. Men, this needs to change.

A Responsibility to Lead

A similar calling is extended to men who aren't married, men who are in dating relationships or who soon will be. To draw a distinction here, a young woman in a dating relationship is not called to depend upon her boyfriend as her primary spiritual leader. Not yet anyway; not before they're married. The boyfriend is still called to be a spiritual leader (or to *become* a spiritual leader), and he's always accountable for his actions. But biblically, the pattern is that a young woman's main spiritual leader is primarily her father (or a Christ-following father figure in her life) before she is married. This is true even if she's a grown woman herself.

Here's an example of why an unmarried woman shouldn't depend on her boyfriend for total spiritual leadership yet.

I (Matt) started walking with Jesus when I was a freshman in college. One evening I met a girl at a church event. We hit it off and started dating. This was the first godly girl I had ever dated. (In high school I'd drifted away from God for a while and had been more interested in worldly girls.) So I met this girl and she loved Jesus. I did too, but she was way ahead of me in terms of spiritual development. On our third date we were sitting across the booth from each other at Chili's restaurant near the Texas A&M campus when she looked at me sort of sideways and said, "Matt, I really like you, and this is just going great. I see what God is doing in your life."

I looked back at her, confused, thinking, *Where is she going with this? Is she going to ask me to marry her?*

Then she locked eyes with me and said, kindly but firmly, "I need you to understand that Jesus is the absolute love of my life, and if you ever touch me in an inappropriate way, I will break up with you *just like that.*" She snapped her fingers.

"Yes ma'am," I said.

Her words shocked me, honestly. I'd never heard anything like that before. Thanks to her leadership, it was a very chaste relationship. But *she* was setting the tone there, not me. I just didn't know any better. That's what I'm talking about here—I was a young Christian guy with no clue about what it meant to lead spiritually. God was extending to me the invitation to lead the relationship spiritually, and that was my calling. But the girl was not depending on me to do it, and a good thing too, because I wasn't there yet.

Here's truth: as men, it's *always* our responsibility to lead in spiritual matters. Although we might not know how, it's up to us to learn how. Find a mentor at church. Begin to meet with a group of godly men for prayer, discipleship, accountability, and Bible study. Accept the awesome responsibility of learning how to point people to Jesus, particularly your future wife.

One of the most beautiful and instructive themes in the Song of Solomon is how the young man in the book carries out all his actions toward the young woman under "the banner of love" (see 2:4). That means the woman felt safe with him. She felt cared for and protected and cherished. Even though the young man and woman were in the throes of a deeply passionate relationship, twice in the book we see the urgent injunction to "not stir up or awaken love until it pleases" (2:7 and 3:5, ESV).

In other words, a big part of sacrificial love (the banner of love) before marriage means putting the brakes on!

Young men, before you marry the girl you're dating, your calling is to treat your girlfriend as if you will one day present her to Jesus as spotless, holy, and completely pure. Any second you spend in sexual activity outside of marriage, you produce the exact opposite of what God has called you to produce in her. Sanctify her. Lead her in spiritual things.

DOWN OFF THE MOUNTAIN

This calling to love sacrificially extends to fathers as well. Not only are we called to be pastors of our wives, but we're called to be pastors of our children too. There's so much in the Bible about being a godly father. One of the main passages is Deuteronomy 6:6–9. If you're a dad, pay close attention. If you're a future dad, let this passage become foundational for you.

To set the scene, Moses is on Mount Sinai meeting with God. While Moses is receiving the commandments, he's enveloped in fire, thick darkness, clouds, thunder, and lightning. All the people of Israel are down at the bottom of the mountain, watching this happen. They know Moses is up there with God, but they don't know any of the specifics of what's going on. All of a sudden, Moses comes hiking down the mountain. He has the Ten Commandments, inscribed on stone tablets, in his arms. Imagine the fear and awe the Israelites felt as Moses climbed down the mountain holding the teachings of almighty God in his arms. That's when they heard this teaching for the first time:

> These words that I command you today shall be on your heart. You
> shall teach them diligently to your children, and shall talk of them when
> you sit in your house, and when you walk by the way, and when you lie
> down, and when you rise. You shall bind them as a sign on your hand,
> and they shall be as frontlets between your eyes. You shall write them on
> the doorposts of your house and on your gates. (ESV)

Seriously, put yourself in that situation. Israel's most famous prophet was telling the Israelites to become teachers of the Word of God themselves. Their primary pupils were to be their children. And he rolls out how to do that. Let's look at the passage again in smaller chunks.

> These words that I command you today shall be on your heart.

That's step one. Let the Word of God be on your heart, Dad. Know the Word of God yourself. The Scripture is not saying you need a seminary degree; it's saying you should be in the Word of God on a regular basis and let it be "on your heart." Pretty simple.

Next...

> You shall teach them diligently to your children, and shall talk of them
> when you sit in your house, and when you walk by the way, and when
> you lie down, and when you rise.

Okay, that's step two, and it's not rocket science either. That simply means you talk about the Bible with your kids. You don't need to know any of the nuances of higher theology or come down hard on the finer points of eschatology.

When do you do it? The Scripture says, "When you sit in your house." Men, when do we sit in our houses? At the dinner table. Just sit down at the dinner table and pause between forkfuls of meatloaf to talk to your kids about

God. This is not hard. If you have little kids, get a book like *The Jesus Storybook Bible*.[1] Open it up, gather your kids around you, and read a story. Ask them questions. If they get a question right (and make sure they get the questions right), they get ice cream. It's that simple. It's that fun.

The same is true for older kids. The Bible says, "When you walk by the way…" In other words, talk about God whenever you're transporting your kids somewhere. Next time your kids are in the car with you, turn the radio off and talk about God. *Annie, John Daniel, tell me about your prayer life. What is God showing you? Are you praying? In what ways can we follow God more closely?*

> When I asked him what wisdom was, he told me it was like having good sense to do the right thing.

When I (Colt) was a kid, my dad would drive me to school if I didn't take the bus. This meant he had a captive audience in the car, and he used those moments to teach me about many things. I remember he told me that it says in Proverbs that every young man who listens to God will receive wisdom. When I asked him what wisdom was, he told me it was like having good sense to do the right thing.

Dad taught me that the Lord grants "good sense" to those who believe in Him, that He protects them and guards their pathways. He taught me that God shows us how to know right from wrong and how to make the right decisions. Our lives are filled with joy when we make the right decisions in life because we have the good sense to not follow dark paths set before us but to follow the right path. Following the path God sets before us, Dad said, is always the way to go.

Those mini Bible lessons made a big impression on me, since I still remember them. I wish now that I'd missed the bus more often.

Next, note that phrase "When you lie down…" What's that talking about? Bedtime. Talk about God when you put your kids to bed. That's not difficult.

Years ago when I (Matt) was a youth pastor, there were two families in the church that I studied closely because the fathers in both situations were doing a great job of leading their families.

In the year 2000 when my first child, John Daniel, was born, I sat both of these dads down separately and asked how they parented as well as they did. They gave several answers apiece, but one answer was the same from both men. They each put their kids to bed, and when they did, they took a few extra minutes to pray, talk about God, and talk about each child's day. In years since, all six kids from both of these families have grown up to be godly men and women. That got my attention.

The idea of being a pastor to your children becomes a little harder when the passage says,

> You shall bind them as a sign on your hand, and they shall be as
> frontlets between your eyes.

What does that mean? This means that as believing fathers, we need to infuse the Word of God into everything we do. Not only does the teaching of the Word of God need to be in our hearts (that's what we just learned), but also the Word of God needs to come out of us in our actions and behavior. Our children need to be able to watch us and know how to live Christian lives where they follow Jesus wholeheartedly.

What's that look like?

Your kids ought to catch you on your knees praying.

Your kids ought to catch you with your Bible open.

Your kids ought to know early what it's like to be prayed for by their father.

Dad, do you realize what an incredibly strong foundation you provide for your children when you pray with them and for them all their growing-up years?

I (Matt) didn't have this luxury. The first time my father and I ever prayed together away from the dinner table was when I was twenty-five years old. It was one of the most beautiful and yet awkward things I've ever done in my life. We were at a Promise Keepers men's conference because I had begged my dad to go with me. At the end of one of the messages, the speaker said, "Okay, dads, this is what we're going to do, maybe some of you for the first time. You're going to pray with your sons." I was ready to go for it, so I literally got down on my knees in the aisle, put my hands on my dad's knee, and started praying. Then it hit me: *I'm twenty-five years old, and I'm praying with my dad for the very first time.* That thought started messing me up, and I started crying.

Now, as a little backstory, my dad is stone deaf. He was a fireman for thirty-seven years, and all those sirens caused him to lose his hearing. So my dad hadn't heard what the speaker had said. He had no idea why in the world I threw myself on the floor, grabbed his knee, and started praying. I think it scared him to death!

We got it all straightened out in the end.

A best-case scenario is that by the time your kids are twenty-five years old, your praying with them should be as natural as walking with them, driving with them, or eating with them around the table. Prayer has become a regular part of who you are with your children.

A True Christ Follower

The key to loving anyone sacrificially is to love Jesus Christ because He first loved you.

This principle works in parenting. Your kids ought to be able to watch you and know what it means to be completely sold out to following Jesus Christ.

This principle works in marriage. You want to have a rock-solid marriage? Be in love with Jesus, and let that love flow through you and affect how you love your wife.

This principle works as a single man. You want to walk in purity with the young women you date? Be in love with Jesus. Follow in the pathway of His commands, and let Him set you free.

The people around you ought to be able to watch you and say, "Oh, that's what it looks like for a grown man to be in love with Jesus."

> This principle works as a single man. You want to walk in purity with the young women you date? Be in love with Jesus.

You might say, "Well, Matt, I don't know about this whole love-for-Jesus thing. I'm just not that emotional of a guy."

I hear this sort of thing all the time from men, and it frustrates me. I even have friends in the ministry who let the men in their church off the hook on this. They say things like, "Men, I know it's uncomfortable, and it's kind of a girl thing to worship."

What?!

What about King David—the same tough guy who killed a heavily armored nine-foot-tall giant with a rock and a slingshot? When David got in the presence of the Lord, he just couldn't contain himself. His arms flew up and he shouted and lost his dignity. He started dancing because he just loved his God (see 2 Samuel 6:14).

Now, no one is saying you need to go to church and act like a teenage girl at a concert. But the point is that we men have a lot more emotions than we admit. What do you get most excited about? Do you ever show emotion when watching sports? Have you ever shouted for joy when your team scored? Did you ever throw your hands in the air with jubilation during a sporting event? Sure you have. Don't tell me you are not emotional. The question then becomes, are you emotional about Jesus?

Listen, if the message of the gospel doesn't move your heart, something is deeply wrong. The truth is that, when you didn't deserve it and when you hadn't earned it, Christ died on a cross to completely pay for your sins. That ought to make you want to shout for joy and throw your hands in the air like the greatest touchdown in history has just been scored. And you ought to be communicating that emotion for God to your wife and children at home.

Let's think for a second about what's at stake. I (Matt) have conducted a lot of funerals of men—funerals of elderly men who were given many years to make the right choices, even funerals of young guys who thought they had their whole lives ahead of them but didn't. I say this without hesitation: there is nothing more pathetic than a man who has lived his life investing in nothing more than his work and his hobbies.

In the end he has nothing. Absolutely nothing.

At the funeral everyone is always so polite. The man's spouse and children and friends stand up and begin to talk about the man who's dead. They say things like, "Well, he was a great guy. Just a great guy. He was a great business-man, and he accomplished a lot in his career, and he was a great leader of this and that. He loved to laugh. He loved golf. He loved fishing. He loved to rock climb."

And then the voices trail off.

They always do. Because there's nothing more to say.

When that happens, I sit on the pew, praying, "Oh, dear Lord, let there be something said about this man, something that points to him living for something that mattered, something of eternal significance." But it doesn't come.

There is nothing more pathetic than that. Everything this man worked for and strived for died with him.

Men, at your funeral, your children and loved ones are going to stand and talk about you. When they speak, they are either going to speak of work and hobbies or they're going to speak of blessing and legacy, of imparting a love for Jesus and the eternal wisdom of God's Word. Which will it be?

Part of the real win for men means we step up to spiritual leadership, just as we step up to leadership in marriage by taking the initiative to love our wives. When we do these things, we can have absolute confidence that we're leading as husbands and fathers the way Christ intended us to. It's a good feeling, be-cause we know we're on the course toward winning.

But what happens when we step out the door of our homes? What happens when we go to work, whether that's on the gridiron, behind a pulpit, in an office, on a factory line, or wherever? It's now time to return to a concept we were introduced to at the end of chapter 2—idolatry. This is a seemingly archaic but actually incredibly relevant concept for the thing we spend most of our waking hours doing, namely, working. It turns out that in our public life in general and our work life in particular, we men need to get our hearts straight with God before we hurt a lot of people. Ourselves included.

What You Care About Most

God wants to be first in our hearts as
we go about the work He has for us.

You shall have no other gods before me.

—Exodus 20:3, esv

Idolatry. God placed an injunction against it as the very first of the Ten Commandments. "You shall have no other gods before me" comes before God telling His people not to murder, steal, lie, commit adultery, or anything else. So we know how serious God was about idolatry.

Idolatry is still a serious problem today, with serious implications. Idolatry occurs anytime we take something and place it in our hearts ahead of God. An idol is anything a man pursues more than he pursues God.

Both of us (Colt and Matt) have struggled with idolatry in the way we pursued success. The success itself wasn't intrinsically wrong, and in many ways we're still hard at work pursuing those same goals. Colt still wants to be the best professional football player he can be. And Matt still wants to be the best pastor he can be.

What's changed is that we both know now that our lives aren't based on those goals. Whether we achieve those goals or not, we won't be shattered or falsely elated either way. Our lives are based on the solid Rock of God, and that's the new definition of success we're pursuing.

But, as mentioned, that's easier said than done—with all of us. Idolatry, one of the greatest obstacles to the real win, is still present right now in men's hearts more than most of us realize and is more destructive to our souls than we could ever dream. So we want to do some more work in this area. Let's take a closer and deeper look at idolatry—and how we can fully rid ourselves of it.[1]

As you read this chapter, think about your life as you live it in relation to other people, especially in the workplace. Do your best to be as honest with yourself as you can be while you consider what your actions say that you value most. Be open to change, if God calls you to that, because until you get this issue right, there can be no progress in your quest for authentic success.

THE GREAT IMMEDIATE NEED

Ask yourself a second time that same question we posed to you at the start of chapter 1. *What do you want in life more than anything else?*

The thing you want is probably not wrong at all. It's probably a good thing, like business success, or a strong marital relationship, or a job that allows you to spend more time with your kids.

But what happens when you don't get what you want? Or what happens when there's a delay in how your prayers are answered? Or when God answers your prayers in ways different than you ever imagined? What then?

That's when we begin to peel back the layers of our lives, get to the root of idolatry, and do some serious work. We begin to see the deepest needs of our hearts—and how Jesus addresses those needs.

Think of it this way. As we said in chapter 2, the reason many of us continually struggle with idolatry is that most of us spend our whole lives looking to noneternal things to meet a need in our hearts that only God can meet. That's why, if you're married, discontentment is prone to pop up in your marriage. It's because you're looking to your wife to meet a need she doesn't have the ability to meet. That's why, if you're a single man, you might be struggling with contentment in your singleness. It's because you're looking to an institution to meet the needs of your heart, but it doesn't have the ability to meet it. That's why you may be discontented with your job or house or car or skills or body. You're looking to a created thing to meet a need that only God can meet.

> Four friends knew that their friend had a great immediate need and that Jesus could meet that need. So they didn't take no for an answer.

Jesus once pointed to the deepest need in a man's heart—and the need looked completely different from what anybody had imagined. Mark 2 records the story. Jesus and His disciples gathered in a house in a town called Capernaum, where Jesus began preaching. A ton of people came to hear Him. So many people, in fact, that the house Jesus preached in was packed. There was no more room for anyone to get in, not even standing by the door.

But four men knew they absolutely had to see Jesus—full house or not. See, their friend was paralyzed. For some reason, he couldn't walk. Maybe he'd been in an accident. Maybe he'd been born that way. For whatever reason, the four friends knew that their friend had a great immediate need and that Jesus could meet that need. So they didn't take no for an answer. House packed? No problem. They climbed to the roof, hauling the paralyzed friend up with them, then removed a section of roof and lowered the friend down.

Question: What was the first thing Jesus said to the guy?

The man's first and greatest need was to walk, wasn't it? You'd expect Jesus to say, "Okay, dude. I see your faith. You're healed. Go for a run." But no. Instead, this is what Jesus said to the paralytic:

Son, your sins are forgiven. (Mark 2:5)

What?!

If you were the paralytic—or any of the four friends for that matter—that's not the answer you'd want to hear. *My sins are forgiven?* You're thinking, *Do You possibly know what it's like not being able to walk? People need to pick me up so I can go to the bathroom. Hey, I appreciate the forgiving-sins thing, but that's not what I really want, Jesus. Do You get that?*

Do we ever take a similar approach with Jesus?

Sure, we approach Him with requests. We ask Him to grant us favors. We want Him to meet the most obvious need we have, like wanting to be mega-church pastors or Rose Bowl MVPs. Or salesman of the month or not going through the divorce or being healed of sickness. But instead Jesus gives something else.

Now in this particular story from the Bible, Jesus eventually does heal the man's legs. But ask yourself, why might Jesus forgive the man's sins before He healed the man's physical needs? It's because Jesus knows something that the paralyzed man and his buddies don't. Jesus knows that this guy has a much deeper need, a longing even greater than his longing to walk.

Think of it this way. If Jesus only healed the man's legs, what would happen? The man would undoubtedly be thrilled. He'd probably go running down the beach beside the Sea of Galilee. The man's life would be changed for the better. But in a couple of months, the euphoria would wear off. The guy would find something else to need, and he would be as discontent as before. If only the physical healing came, then only the physical need would be met, but the spiritual need wouldn't.

That's why Jesus didn't fulfill the guy's need to walk first. He fulfilled a much deeper need first—a longing the man had for his heart to be filled with what mattered eternally.

DEEP INSIDE

Go back to that same question again. Ask yourself: What has your heart been longing for? If you said business success or a strong marital relationship or a job that allows you to spend more time with your kids or whatever, there's actually a deeper answer, one that you need to uncover if you're ever going to move on and go toward the real win.

The twist is this. What your heart has been longing for is actually much deeper than the desire that seems most pressing. There's no one place in Scripture that comes right out and defines the list of idols in our lives. But it's a fact that we as humans have taken a billion things and let them take the place of God in our lives. We believe there are at least four common, major idols in the lives of men, and we'll be getting to them shortly.

> Ask yourself:
> What has your heart
> been longing for?

Regardless of what the biggest idols in your life are, if you desire the real win, that means grabbing a shovel and going to work on your heart. You've got to dig past the surface layers and expose the problems underneath. When those problems are laid bare, you can confess them to the Lord, allow His Spirit to begin to work on your life in new and real ways, and go forward with true success. This kind of heart work is often best done within community, either with the help of a trusted friend or with a men's group at church. ·

Now let's take a look at the four main idols:

1. The idol of power

The desire for power is huge in the hearts of men. Now power isn't necessarily bad. After all, power is the capability to accomplish something great and influence others positively. But when people worship this idol, it's like saying, "I have worth when I have influence, recognition, and fame. I'm important because I can cause people to do what I want, when I want, exactly as I want it done."

Here's how you know if you've made power an idol in your life:

- You desire authority over people. You need to be in charge.
- Your greatest fear is humiliation.
- You easily feel disrespected.

- You hate it when you tell someone to do something and he does something else. You feel a great need to call the shots, whether at work, at home, at church, or in a relationship. When you talk, people need to move.
- You struggle with giving credit to others. And if others do not give you what you consider proper recognition, then you get angry or jealous.
- You hate to have people question you or your decisions. You feel slighted or maligned when people do.
- You don't have a huge desire to control the future, but you long to be highly influential in it.

Here's what repentance from a power idol looks like:

- You are not driven anymore by the need to have authority over others. You are content in knowing that the Holy Spirit is the true authority in people's lives.
- If somebody gets credit for something you did, you're okay with that. Your value comes from the Lord, not from the power you hold over other people.
- When you expect somebody to do something and he doesn't, you're okay with that. You recognize that God may be calling that person to something different from your wishes.
- The deepest motivation of your heart is to bring recognition to God, not recognition for yourself.
- You truly believe and act on the words of Jesus when He says in Matthew 23:11–12, "The greatest among you shall be your servant. Whoever exalts himself will be humbled, and whoever humbles himself will be exalted" (ESV).

2. The idol of control

To control something means you regulate it or restrain it. In the right situation, for someone who has the right authority, control might be a good or even necessary thing. But some people feel a need to know exactly what's happening or a need to guarantee a certain outcome, when in fact they don't have any such need. When people worship this idol, it's like saying, "I'm only content and happy and at peace if I am able to get mastery over a certain area in my life or if things are occurring according to my plans or my desires."

Here's how you know when control has become an idol in your life:

- If things don't go as planned or expected, you experience fear, anger, or anxiety in your heart.
- If you have set a schedule in your mind but somebody deviates from your schedule, you feel frustrated or stressed out.
- A lack of organization causes an unhealthy amount of fear, anger, or exasperation in you.
- If your child has a school project, you do it for him.
- For you as a parent, if something threatens the future of your kids, you feel like you're unraveling.
- It's a struggle for you to let anyone lead except yourself.
- You struggle with giving to the church because you don't trust the church leadership God has put in place or you don't have a say in where the money is spent.
- You obsess over things such as the stock market or your retirement account or a future job or getting married. You have five-year plans, but these things won't neatly fit into those plans.
- Your budget, instead of being a guideline for healthy spending and saving, becomes a tyrant, and you experience arguments and disunity in your marriage if your spouse deviates from it.

Here's what repentance from a control idol looks like:

- When life becomes chaotic, either in the little everyday stuff or in the big trials of life, you don't spiral into fear and frustration. You trust in God and in His ultimate sovereignty over all.
- You truly believe that your life's schedule is not the same thing as God's. God operates on His own schedule, and you trust His timing.

- Your heart is at rest in the sovereignty of God over your present and your future.
- You believe the words of Jesus in Matthew 6:31, 33 when He says, "Do not be anxious.… But seek first the kingdom of God and his righteousness, and all these things will be added to you" (ESV).
- You act upon Proverbs 3:5–6: "Trust in the LORD with all your heart, and do not lean on your own understanding. In all your ways acknowledge him, and he will make straight your paths" (ESV).

3. The idol of comfort

Comfort is the feeling of being soothed, consoled, relieved, or reassured. We all need comfort sometimes. But some people seek comfort as a right or out of some kind of inner compulsion. If this is your idol, you don't feel content, at peace, or happy unless you experience a certain quality of life or a particular pleasure.

Here's how you know if you've made comfort an idol:

- You are driven by securing a life that is easier, not harder.
- Avoiding stress and difficulty has become a primary motivating factor in your life.
- In order to comfort yourself in times of stress and trial, you tend to turn first to things such as food, pornography or other illicit sexual pleasure, entertainment, or "me time" instead of to the Lord.

Here's what repentance from the idol of comfort looks like:

- You acknowledge that discomfort is a necessary part of life.
- You believe that if God wants you to work your fingers to the bone or be poor for the rest of your life, that's okay, because desiring Jesus is better than desiring comfort.
- You start looking at money primarily as a resource to advance the kingdom, not primarily as a resource to fund your lifestyle.
- When you feel the chaos and stress of life closing in, you don't turn first to TV or sex or porn; you turn first to Jesus.

- If you're single, you value your girlfriend's holiness more than you do your physical needs.
- You believe in your heart that the highest pleasure is found in Jesus. As Psalm 16:11 says, "You make known to me the path of life; in your presence there is fullness of joy; at your right hand are pleasures forevermore" (ESV).

4. The idol of approval

Approval is when people praise you, judge you favorably, agree with you, or consistently commend you for a job well done. Who doesn't want approval? But the desire for others' approval can get out of hand. When approval is your idol, you're not content or at peace unless you are loved or accepted by a particular person or group of people.

Here's how you know if you've made approval an idol:

- If you do, say, or write something and ten people compliment you but one person makes a negative or offhanded comment, your day is ruined. All you can think about is that one negative comment.
- If someone unfriends you on Facebook or Twitter, you are really bothered. Or if you write something on Facebook or Twitter or a blog, you constantly look to see if people are responding.
- If you find out that you aren't invited to some event, it ruins your day.
- If you're single, you feel unloved.
- If you're single, you won't stand up for holiness in the physical area of your dating relationship because you're afraid your girlfriend will be disappointed in you.

Here's what it looks like to repent of the idol of approval:

- You value God's approval more than anyone else's.
- When you find out somebody doesn't like you or says something negative about you, your day isn't ruined because you know your heavenly Father cares for you deeply.

- If you are married, when your wife doesn't pursue you physically, you don't turn to porn. Instead, you turn to Jesus, resting in the approval and the love of the Lord. You cherish and serve your wife anyway.
- If you are single, you don't feel unloved or even unfulfilled, because you are content with the love of Christ and His plan for your life.

It's one thing to identify an idol, and it's something altogether different to lay down that idol and give your heart completely to Jesus. God has spoken. He said, "Have no other gods before me." That's a powerful statement, and our response needs to be to come to Jesus today. As the story of the paralyzed man shows, Jesus may or may not change your immediate circumstances. But when you come to Him, He will always do something better for you. He'll fulfill the deepest desires of your heart!

So how does God go about healing the idolatry in our hearts? The good news is that God is going to remove the idols from your heart.

Free from Idols, Free to Love God

God loves you too much for you to spend your entire life pursuing something that does not have the ability to satisfy you. Philippians 1:6 says, "I am confident of this very thing, that He who began a good work in you will perfect it until the day of Christ Jesus" (NASB). The promise of Scripture is that, from the day you are saved, every day until you see Him face to face, He is perfecting the work He began in you and transforming you so you are more like Jesus.

There are a couple of ways God goes about removing the idols from the heart of a man.

One, if you're His child and if there is something you have made an idol, He will remove that idol in your life by not letting you get that thing your heart wants so badly. By not giving you what your heart has made an idol, He will turn your heart to Him so that you'll realize that He's enough for you. God may be withholding a really good thing that you desire until you get to the place where you truly believe that He is enough.

I (Colt) told you in chapter 1 about the heartbreaking way an injury took me out of the college National Championship game—a game my team went on to lose. The truth is, prior to that point in my life, winning that game had become an idol to me. It was the most important thing in my life. At that time it was practically all I thought about or cared about.

I'm not saying that God vindictively caused me to get that injury. But I do believe He said something to me as a result of it. I believe He said, "Colt, let this wake you up. I know you wanted to win that game and hold up that trophy, and that would have been a great feeling for you. But maybe this will show you that football's not the most important thing in your life. Let this wake you up to realize that *I'm* the most important thing in your life."

> Winning that game had become an idol to me. It was the most important thing in my life. At that time it was practically all I thought about or cared about.

As a result of having something I'd wanted all my life up to that point taken out of my reach, I realized an important truth. I realized that if football were gone, if everything I owned were removed from me, if everything I ever worked for were taken away, God would still be enough for me. Prior to the National Championship, I couldn't have said that. Not honestly, anyway. Not really understanding it and owning it. But I believe it now with all my heart. All because my idol was yanked away from me in an instant.

So that's the first way God removes the idol from the heart of a man—He lets you experience the loss of what you desire too much to have.

Two, He will actually let you have that thing that you are looking for in order to fill some longing in your heart. He'll give it to you to prove that it actually can't meet your heart's desire; only He can. Just like what happened to

King Solomon. You'll say, "Nothing on earth will ever fill the longing of my heart except God."

That's what my (Matt's) story was. Unlike Colt and his college championship, the Lord didn't withhold from me the idol I was lifting up—the approval of the world. He gave it to me, and it still wasn't enough. It didn't matter how big my church grew, it would still crush me if one of the members left. It didn't matter how many times people would say, "Thanks, your sermon ministered to me," because if one person would walk up and say, "I don't like your preaching," it would just mess me up.

Then one of the biggest breakthroughs God has ever made toward healing my idol of approval happened a few years back. One of our other teaching pastors was preaching about Jacob, who kept running from God. The pastor said, "No matter how many times Jacob let go of God, God never let go of Jacob," and for some reason the light bulb came on. God spoke so clearly to my heart in that moment. It was like God was saying, "Matt, you've let go of Me and run away from Me ten thousand times before, but I've never let go of you." And it hit me so strongly that God loves me and approves of me.

These days, when somebody criticizes me, it doesn't crush me. When you've truly felt the approval of the Lord, the approval of people just doesn't matter that much. Now, when I receive the approval or applause or recognition of people, it ministers to me, but I know in my heart that it just doesn't compare to the applause of Jesus. There's nothing compared to the love and approval of Jesus.

A quote from pastor and speaker Joseph Stowell has ministered to me greatly. This quote points to the real win, and I hold it out to you as an invitation.

I'm only in my early sixties, and I already find myself weary of the hollow memories of what few accomplishments I may have mustered in my life. My failures continue to embarrass me. The inadequacies I have carried with me since my youth still frustrate me. My insecurities still trouble my soul. And the praise of others has an increasingly hollow ring. I am tired of worrying about whether or not the sermon I preached was good enough or whether or not someone will pat me on the back for a job well done. I'm tired of worrying about what people think about me. I'm weary of the carnal feeling that sometimes haunts me when someone talks about their favorite preacher…and it's not me.

Bottom line, I just flat out get tired of me. But I never get tired of Jesus.

After all these years, I still find Him more compelling, more engaging, more awesome, more surprising, more fulfilling, and more attractive than ever before.

I never get tired of singing His praises or of watching Him perform. I find Him to be gripping. Absorbing. Beyond comprehension. And that's why—along with Paul, my grandmother, Billy Graham, and countless others through the years—I find myself longing to know Him better.

Can you relate to this? I can. This is what it's like when you put God before every other possible "god" in your life, including your job.

Stowell goes on to describe the blessings of getting rid of the idols in our lives so that we can love the one true God above all.

I am becoming increasingly aware that life doesn't go on forever. When we're young, we think we're bulletproof. We live like we'll never die. But when your knees protest certain movements and your eyesight and memory begin to grow fuzzy, reality sets in. Time moves us on, and before long we all will be on the edge of life in the past tense, with most of our days in the rearview mirror.

As much as I would rather not think about it, the day is coming when I'll be sitting in the corner of some nursing home waiting for them to ring the lunch bell. And if life up to that point has been all about me, that is going to be a sad and empty day—no matter what they're serving for lunch. Why? Because all I will have will be me! Which at that point won't be much.

But…if my life has been about knowing Jesus and experiencing a deepening relationship with Him, as I sit in that corner of the nursing home waiting for the lunch bell to ring, He'll be there with me.

And He'll be more wonderful on that day than ever before. His presence will be my companion. He'll talk with me, and I won't have any trouble hearing Him when He tells me that I am His own. He'll say, "Well, Joe, you're almost home." And I'll say, "Lord, the sooner the better. I've heard Your voice through all these years, and now I can't wait to see Your face." [2]

It's not easy to root out the idols of our hearts, to confess them to the Lord, and to walk forward in true success. But it's God's call on your life.

God is inviting you to stand on all the promises of His Word. His way is always better, and He promises a life of absolute confidence to those who follow His ways. When your heart and mind are set on Christ, you're standing on the Rock.

As we move on, let's get very practical. Let's look more specifically at an area that all men grapple with over the course of their lives. It's something we're encouraged to do "heartily," as we'll see next.

Choose Your Boss

Working to please God
transforms every man's job.

> Whatever you do, work heartily, as for the
> Lord and not for men.
>
> —COLOSSIANS 3:23, ESV

People usually see professional football players only on game days—
Sundays. But have you ever wondered what guys like me (Colt) do during the
rest of the week?

On Mondays, during the regular season, we have practice. We watch the
weekend's game and review tapes, then start preparing for the next game.

Tuesday is our day off, our "weekend," although a few players show up for
a couple of hours on Tuesdays. I'm one of them. As a quarterback, I often go in
on Tuesdays for a good portion of the day to get a head start on the week, so I
know what our game plan is going to be.

For the rest of the week, every player is all in. We practice Wednesday
through Friday. On Saturdays, we're often traveling if there's an away game, so
we have a crisp walk-through in the morning. Sunday is game day. If we're
away, we travel back home afterward.

And it all starts all over again. Monday is another practice. Tuesday is another day off. And so on.

The average practice looks different depending on whether you play offense or defense. Since I'm a quarterback, my day is full every day. I get to the facility about 6:00 a.m., have breakfast, look over what we're going to do for the day, then watch some film—either of our previous day's practice or of our upcoming opponent. We have our regular team meeting at nine. Then we'll break down and go into other specific meetings for either offense or defense. I meet with the offensive line, the receivers, and the running backs. Then we'll do a walk-through of the next set of drills and plays at eleven.

At noon we have lunch. Right after lunch, everybody will get taped up, and we'll go out on the field for practice. We'll practice for ninety minutes to two hours, then come back in and have more meetings. We'll watch the day's practice and talk about corrections we need to make in preparation for Sunday.

Right after the debriefing is finished, I go to the weight room. (Or if I'm injured, I go into the training room for treatment.) I lift weights year-round since I'm not blessed with the classic quarterback 6-foot 5-inch, 230-pound frame. I'm just under 6 feet 2 inches, and I like to play at around 220 pounds. So I need to work out and eat to maintain my size and muscle mass. That means I constantly spend time in the weight room.

I go home around 6:00 each evening. The running joke is that after Halloween I never see the sun. I get to the facility early in the morning and leave at night, so it's always dark when I'm outside. For me, work means a long day, every day. I'm not just a guy who walks out onto the field on Sunday, plays a game, then does nothing the rest of the week. Just like you, I work, and it's tough. It can even be a grind. I bet your job is similar in the sense that you encounter difficulty and challenges.

> You may be wondering how anything good at all can come from the kind of job you have.

Work is something we'll do most of our lives. So how can we find purpose, joy, and value in the work God has called us to do? This subject affects pretty much every man over the age of fifteen. Anything God has you doing is considered work, whether you're a full-fledged career man, a student, or a guy who is just beginning in the work force flipping burgers in a fast-food restaurant.

What's your job like? And how does God define winning when it comes to your work? The clue to the answer is in the Bible verse quoted at the start of this chapter: we're to work for God and not for men. That's easier to say than it is to really understand. And it's easier to understand than it is to actually do. But this chapter is here to help you.

First, though, you may be wondering how anything good at all can come from the kind of job you have. If you hate your job, you're far from alone.

When You Hate Your Job

Awhile back, I (Matt) read a book called *Open,* the autobiography of Andre Agassi, the great tennis star of the last couple of decades. Listen to how he describes his work.

> My name is Andre Agassi. My wife's name is Stefanie Graf. We have two children, a son and a daughter, five and three. We live in Las Vegas, Nevada, but currently reside in a suite at the Four Seasons Hotel in New York City, because I'm playing in the 2006 U.S. Open. My last U.S. Open. In fact my last tournament ever. I play tennis for a living, even though I hate tennis, hate it with a dark and secret passion, and always have.[1]

Isn't that fascinating? I picked up the book in an airport bookstore. That quote was on the first page, and it instantly grabbed me. Look at the last line of the quote again: "I play tennis for a living, even though I hate tennis, hate it with a dark and secret passion, and always have."

Truth be told, that's how many men feel about their work. Maybe even you. Could this be your quote?

Hi, my name is _____, and I do XYZ for a living, even though I hate XYZ, hate it with a dark and secret passion, and always have.

Other men don't necessarily hate their jobs this intensely, but deep down they're struggling with the greater purpose of their jobs. They wonder, what's this really all for? Does my work have any eternal significance? Am I wasting my life with this thing I currently do?

You may be in college right now, working hard in preparation for a career. You're giving the best hours of your life to making good grades so you can get a job. That career direction seems hope-filled, but perhaps one day in the near future you too will hate your work with a dark and secret passion. Or you might enjoy your job, but deep down you wonder if working sixty hours a week is worth it, particularly because the only tangible benefit you see from all your hard work is that your company's CEO owns a third home in the Virgin Islands.

No matter what Andre Agassi says about his job, there's good news when it comes to a man's career path. Following God means we don't need to hate our work, even if what we do isn't fun or inspiring. God invites us to follow Him wholeheartedly in every area of our lives, including what we do for a living. The Scriptures have a lot to say about how we are to approach, view, and find purpose in work.

Genesis 2 is a key passage, setting the stage for a right understanding of this all-important area of our lives. Even at the dawn of time, man was put to work in the Garden of Eden.

The LORD God formed the man of dust from the ground and breathed into his nostrils the breath of life, and the man became a living creature.

And the LORD God planted a garden in Eden, in the east, and there he put the man whom he had formed…. The LORD God took the man and put him in the garden of Eden to work it and keep it. (Genesis 2:7–8, 15, ESV)

The Bible is clear. This is man's God-established purpose from the beginning of time: to work. God placed man in the Garden of Eden to cultivate and keep it.

Note that this placement happened before the Fall. This means work is not evil. It's God-ordained. Before man ever sinned, God put him in the garden and put him to work.

Don't go any farther until you catch the significance of that fact. See, somehow in my nearly four decades of going to church, eighteen years of Sunday school as a kid, eight years of going to college and getting my master's degree, and fifteen-plus years of preaching, I got it wrong. I thought that work didn't come into the picture until after Adam and Eve sinned, so in my mind, work was a punishment. Somehow I had it backward, thinking that before the Fall the man and woman just lay around all day and kind of chilled, ate fruit, and hung out naked. But the truth is that they were working, even back then. And it was a good thing.

But there's more to the story. Because, you see, the Fall *did* happen. And it changed man's relationship to work forever.

Genesis 3:17–19, a post-Fall passage, lays out a key part of the effects that the curse for the original sin would have on mankind. God says to Adam,

Because you have listened to the voice of your wife
    and have eaten of the tree
of which I commanded you,
    "You shall not eat of it,"
cursed is the ground because of you;
    in pain you shall eat of it all the days of your life;

thorns and thistles it shall bring forth for you;

   and you shall eat the plants of the field.

By the sweat of your face

   you shall eat bread,

till you return to the ground,

   for out of it you were taken;

for you are dust,

   and to dust you shall return. (ESV)

So let's contrast the image of work given in Scripture before the Fall to the image of work seen after the Fall.

Before sin, work was a part of Adam's day that he enjoyed. It wasn't a burden to him. Work was what gave man a goal. It provided purpose and fulfillment. Man's work environment was a lush garden filled with animals he named and plants he tended.

After sin, work became burdensome and difficult. Man's work environment was a field filled with thistles, thorns, and sweat. Work had the capacity to feel difficult, fruitless, pointless, and purposeless. That's why, thousands of years later, one of the best tennis players of all time, a career athlete who made hundreds of millions of dollars playing tennis (not to mention inspiring thousands of fans the world over), would describe his work so negatively. "I play tennis for a living, even though I hate tennis, hate it with a dark and secret passion, and always have."

Now, maybe you think Andre Agassi is an exception to the rule. Maybe he's just weird because he used to have funny hair and wear acid-washed blue jean shorts. But the curse of the Fall affects every man's work, including ours today. Check out what one of the wisest men who has ever lived had to say about work. Solomon, in Ecclesiastes 2:4–7, 10–11, describes work with the same dismay as Agassi does.

I made great works. I built houses and planted vineyards for myself. I

made myself gardens and parks, and planted in them all kinds of fruit trees. I made myself pools from which to water the forest of growing trees…. I had also great possessions of herds and flocks, more than any who had been before me in Jerusalem….

I kept my heart from no pleasure, for my heart found pleasure in all my toil, and this was my reward for all my toil. Then I considered all that my hands had done and the toil I had expended in doing it, and behold, all was vanity and a striving after wind, and there was nothing to be gained under the sun. (ESV)

See the last line of that quote? That's how the wisest man on the planet described all his fabulous work—like chasing wind. Have you ever chased wind? Go chase it sometime and see how successful you are at catching it.

So this is what Scripture is teaching (and it doesn't matter what you do for a living) about work after the Fall: On your most financially profitable year, during your greatest year of productivity, during the season of your career when you are most applauded and promoted and find the most joy in your work, if you haven't discovered a God-ordained purpose for your days, then you are laboring in vain!

That's what a job outside the Garden of Eden looks like. Futility! You're spending your whole life chasing after wind. No matter how good you are at what you do, no matter how much money you make at it, no matter how many awards or promotions or accolades you receive, you will eventually discover what Andre Agassi and King Solomon both discovered.

All your work has been for nothing. And if that's all your work ever is to you—work—it will produce in you a dark hatred.

Redeeming Work from the Fall

Fortunately, there is good news—the news of redemption. The gospel of Jesus Christ and the message of His cross give purpose and value and joy back to a man's work. Because of the gospel, you no longer work in vain. Because of the work of the cross, you no longer chase after the wind. Jesus Christ redeems work, and that changes everything. Work is no longer futile. It's purposeful again. Colossians 1:19–20 says,

> In [Christ] all the fullness of God was pleased to dwell, and through
> him to reconcile to himself all things, whether on earth or in heaven,
> making peace by the blood of his cross. (ESV)

Think of Jesus "reconciling" things to God as redeeming things. He's making them purposeful in God. Thanks to the redemption that Christ provides—not only the redemption of our souls but also the redemption of our life purpose—our work can become infused with meaning and even joy.

But this win isn't handed to us on a platter. We participate with God in attaining it. Consider three ways you can infuse joy and purpose back into the work God has given you to do.

1. Whatever work you do right now is God's will for you in this moment. Embrace it.

God has determined every person's appointed times and boundaries of habitation (Acts 17:26). That means wherever you are in life, whatever you are doing, God has set it in motion. Your job is a part of God's perfect plan for your life right now.

Now that doesn't mean you can't desire to do something different. It just means that for you to begin to find joy, purpose, and value in what you do, you need to understand that you are not where you are today by accident.

God in His sovereignty decided that on this particular day and year, you would be living right where you are living, doing exactly what you are doing. When you put it through that grid, then your job takes on new meaning. When you realize that God handpicked you to be manager of these people, or God handpicked you to be the teacher of this classroom, or God handpicked you to be the boss of this corporation, or God handpicked you to dig this ditch, then you're reaching the real win. You can be absolutely confident that you are exactly where God wants you to be. Your job isn't at the center of your life. God is. And He has ordained and orchestrated you to be doing the job you are right now.

Tell it to yourself this way. *If God has placed me here, and if God's hand has determined this, then He must have something important, purposeful, and valuable that He wants me to do.*

> That means you don't work for your boss.... You work *for God.*

That means you don't work for your boss. Not ultimately. God chose you. God placed you in this position. Therefore…

You work *for God.*

Which brings us to the second way we can discover and infuse joy and purpose back into the work that God has given us to do.

2. Whatever you do, work heartily, as for the Lord and not for men.

This second point comes straight from Scripture—Colossians 3:23, esv. It doesn't matter if you're the CEO of a Fortune 500 company or the low man in an organization making paper clips; God invites you to work heartily for Him. That means when it comes to your job, your call is to give it everything you've got. Why? Again, because God placed you here for a reason, He must have a purpose for you. You're working for God, not a person, so work as if God were the only One you need to please.

It can be tempting in various work situations to give less than 100 percent. Have you ever been there before? I know I've encountered that temptation. Working less than 100 percent means you do as little as you can to get by, unless someone is watching. Or you appear to be busy even if you aren't. You appear to be indispensable to the company when you're really not. Or you take credit for as many ideas as you can, even when they're not all yours. It's also tempting, no matter what job you're at, to jockey for position or look to your employer as your ultimate source of income and security.

But Scripture says we are to work from the soul with everything we've got, not as if we were working for man, but for the Lord.

When you realize you are working for the Lord, you're not going to do as little as you can; you're going to do more than you need to—even when no one is watching. Why? Because you are working for your King. You're working to please Him. You're not going to take credit for as much as you possibly can either. You'll actually begin to elevate the people around you, because "God opposes the proud but gives grace to the humble" (James 4:6, NIV). You're not going to jockey for position. You're going to "work heartily, as for the Lord" (Colossians 3:23, ESV) and trust that God will elevate you when He feels your character is ready for that elevation. Within your work, you're going to rest because you know that your company is not the ultimate source of income and security. God is. Knowing that will bring a confidence and peace like you've never imagined.

Now for the third way we can discover and infuse joy and purpose back into the work that God has given us to do.

3. Wherever you work, you can find purpose and joy in your work by finding the eternal value in what you do.

Some work has obvious eternal value. Some doesn't. The challenge is to find eternal value no matter what you do for a living.

A passage that, surprisingly, points men this way is Ephesians 4:28:

> He who steals must steal no longer; but rather he must labor, performing with his own hands what is good, so that he will have something to share with one who has need. (NASB)

Did you catch how crazy that is? This verse instructs a thief to quit his thieving ways and work instead. Not surprising so far. But the verse doesn't stop there. The thief is told to go forward and, instead of stealing, do something eternally significant with his time, energy, and talents. Instead of stealing, he's supposed to work so that he can share with those who are in need.

If that is the high standard a thief is held to, how much greater are the standards for you and me?

When I think of high standards, I think of Jesse Reeves, a good friend of mine who helped us plant Austin Stone Church. He's a phenomenal musician—Chris Tomlin's bass player and cowriter. Earlier on in his music career, Jesse was talking with Neil McClendon, the same pastor who phoned me when I had cancer and told me to live with unction. Neil asked Jesse to define success. Now by this time, Jesse had some answers but was still working it out too. So Neil laid it on the line, same as he did for me.

> How can I use this job that God has placed me in to make an eternal difference?

He said, "Jesse, if all you've done at the end of your life is sold a bunch of CDs, then you've made a huge spiritual fumble. If that happens, one day you're going to stand before Jesus, and He's going to look at you and say, 'Too small.'"

By contrast, Neil encouraged Jesse to write songs that people could use to glorify God with, as well as to raise up and disciple others to be leaders, lovers of God, and excellent musicians. In other words, Neil was trying to get Jesse to really dig down and ask a question of himself: *What can I do through* this *job that will be eternally significant? How can I use this job that God has placed me in to make an eternal difference?*

Jesse took Neil's advice to heart. He now pours himself out in discipling people, and he went on to cowrite "How Great Is Our God," one of the most widely circulated and influential worship songs of our generation.

Ask yourself that same question. Imagine that you are standing before the Lord today and He asks you, "What are you accomplishing through your work that has eternal significance?" What would your answer be? And would that answer give Him cause to say, "Too small" or "Well done"?

Finding eternal significance in your work might require a bit of discovery as you pray it out before the Lord. Certainly, all work is important because it's part of God's purpose for your life. But as Neil was saying, there is more than just getting up each morning, coming home each evening, and collecting a paycheck.

When you know in your heart of hearts that God has you in the job you're in for a reason, and when you work from your soul with everything you've got as if you're working for God and not men, then you're on your way. Pray through and think about how God can use you for eternal impact through what you do. You're standing on the Rock then.

THE IMPORTANCE OF PARTNERSHIP

Both of us (Matt and Colt) want to offer a specific word to married men here when it comes to work. If you're not married, pay attention, because understanding this perspective will help you greatly if and when you get married one day. (And we've got a special point to make for you coming up.)

The specific word to you if you are a married man has to do with your work and your wife. The Scripture shows that when God created woman, life got really good and really complicated—at the same time. And a big part of that complication has to do with each gender's specific roles and purposes in life.

Let's go back to the story of Eden to pick up one of the most powerful verses in Scripture: Genesis 2:18. It tells us a lot about having a partner in our work.

> The LORD God said, "It is not good that the man should be alone; I will make him a helper fit for him." (ESV)

A few verses earlier, we find that God had pronounced as "very good" everything He had made in creation (Genesis 1:31). But now we find out there was an exception. One thing was "not good"—the first man was alone. God Himself lived in community as Father, Son, and Holy Spirit, so He knew how desperately important it was that man be in community with other creatures similar to himself.

Now, by saying it wasn't good that the first man was alone, God wasn't implying that it is always horrible when a man (or woman) is single. From the rest of Scripture, we know that singles are complete and valuable and fulfilled without having a spouse. Singleness is not a curse. In fact, we know from Scripture that singleness is actually a gift (see 1 Corinthians 7:7–8).

God didn't create the first woman to *complete* the first man. He created her to *help* him.

Now, in case that sounds like a subservient position, let us point out that it isn't. Sure, there's always a temptation when people hear the word "helper" to think that means second-class citizen or sidekick. But those things are not the meaning of the word. To be called a "helper" is actually to be placed in excellent company. In Scripture, three very important Persons are described as helpers: God the Father (Psalm 121:1–2), Jesus (1 John 2:1), and the Holy Spirit (John 14:16–18).

Look carefully again at Genesis 2:18. Why did God create Eve? Here it is: "I will make him a *helper fit* for him" (ESV). The Scripture does not say, "It is not good for man to be alone, so I will make him a companion for him." Nor does the Scripture say, "It is not good for man to be alone, so I will make him somebody to hang around with." The Scripture defines the match as a suitable partnership, a good fit. Two can do the work better than one.

> Are women equal to men? Yes. Do women have unique and specific callings on their lives? Yes.

God created Eve to help Adam fulfill the calling that God had placed on Adam's life.

Now let me just say this right now, so you don't have to e-mail me later. Are women equal to men? Yes. Do women have unique and specific callings on their lives? Yes. Do women have their own gifting essential to the body of Christ? Absolutely.

But the role of the wife to the husband is clear. When a woman gets married, one of the primary callings on her life is for her to come alongside her husband and help him fulfill the calling that God has given him. A marriage creates a new team, and a calling becomes a married couple's calling together.

A Huge Warning

Now, one obvious question to ask is, how exactly can a wife be a helper? It doesn't mean that both people in a marriage need to do the same job. As a matter of fact, we're actually not going to answer that question directly. Instead we want to go the other direction as we close this chapter, and offer a strong warning about what can happen when a husband and wife aren't on the same page when it comes to a calling. That might sound really strange, but there's a good reason for it, we promise.

Awhile back, I (Matt) had a conversation with a guy considered to be one of the premier marriage counselors in the country. He said that in his more than thirty years of dealing with affairs, he found that about 90 percent of them originated from relationships that men and women have in the context of work.[2] I asked why.

He explained how it goes back to man being placed in the garden. God made Adam a helper to come alongside him and help fulfill God's purpose and calling on his life. Through that mutual, side-by-side fulfilling of God's purposes together comes companionship, community, closeness, intimacy, and purpose.

Consider the point raised by the marriage counselor again, and turn it into a question: Why do so many affairs occur at work?

It's because a man and a woman are laboring together toward a common cause.

See, when this happens, a man and a woman are simulating a relationship that God designed for a husband and a wife to share together. Now, to be clear, it's not wrong for women and men to work together. It's unavoidable, and when it's done well, it's a beautiful picture of the body of Christ working together. But make no mistake; when a woman and a man are working together for a common cause, it produces connectedness and even a sense of intimacy. God designed it to. That's why work-related relationships are prone to spiral into emotional or physical affairs.

If you're working with a woman who's not your wife, the real win comes when you set strong and clear boundaries on your relationship together. Maybe this sounds extreme, but then maybe we *need* to get extreme in this area. Think of how many amazing men and women of God have derailed their lives and ministries by not setting boundaries. If you think it could never happen to you, be forewarned. Plenty of godly people thought the same thing…right before falling big-time into this sin.

When it comes to setting boundaries, here are some wise principles to follow:

- Never be alone with a female workmate. If it can at all be avoided, never ride together, eat lunch together, travel together as just the two of you, or spend extended time in the office working alone together.
- Keep all conversations work related and surface level. Don't ask a female coworker about any subjects of depth, including her marriage or walk with the Lord. That's her husband's job, not yours.
- Don't compliment her on the way she looks. That's also her husband's job, not yours.
- If you have a friendship with a female coworker, express that friendship only when your wife is around.
- Never be friends with a woman who your wife is not friends with also.

Because I (Matt) have personally taken this stance toward women, I sometimes get accused of being standoffish. But I would rather be standoffish than adulterous.

If you work in close proximity to somebody of the opposite sex, it's okay. Just guard your heart—and hers too. Create workable but appropriate boundaries in every interaction. Work with excellence, as for the Lord, not to impress anyone, including female coworkers. And allow no foothold in your life for the enemy to exploit.

A Final Word for Single Men

Now we want to offer a word directly to single men. If you're single, let's shoot straight for a moment when it comes to what qualities to look for in who you marry. (If you're married, chances are good that you have a friend who's single, so consider passing this along to him.)

One of the biggest reasons divorce is so rampant today is because people get married for the wrong reasons. People seek attraction, companionship, and compatibility first, not calling. But what Genesis 2:18 shows us is that calling must be central to a healthy relationship. You don't need to do the same job as the person you marry, but it's important to be heading in the same direction. You need to have an understanding of the overarching calling of your life. Let a shared mutual calling to Christ and a desire to fulfill His purposes together be foundational to your marriage.

I (Colt) fell in love with my wife for many reasons. I admit that, initially, I was attracted to Rachel's looks. But over time, her servant heart and commitment to the same calling that I had made me fall in love with her more deeply than ever. Not only do I know she loves Jesus more than anything, but I know that she has understood from the beginning of our commitment to each other that being the wife of an NFL quarterback was going to be tough on her. But she felt that God had called her to walk alongside me as I fulfill this calling for the current season of my life.

Single men, the number-one thing to look for in the girl you hope to marry is not physical attraction or whether she's funny or smart or has a good job or is a good dresser. It's that she's in love with Jesus and that you have a clear sense that God has handpicked her to come alongside you and help you fulfill God's call on your life.

Both of us (Colt and Matt) have seen from experience that too many godly single men compromise in this area. They find a girl who only sorta loves Jesus and is only sorta committed to her calling in Christ. But they stay with her anyway because she is so attractive. If that's where you're headed, keep this in mind: ten years down the road, when she leaves you because she loves herself more than she loves Jesus, you will discover anew the warning Solomon discovered for himself several thousand years ago.

Charm is deceptive, and beauty is fleeting. (Proverbs 31:30, NIV)

If you are single right now, pray that God would reveal to you the right person for you to walk through life with and serve God with. If you find someone, but she is not committed to living in God's call and purpose, then do not marry her. If she isn't following Jesus with everything she's got, you'll be marrying a little piece of hell on earth.

Men, set your eyes on Jesus and run for Him with everything you got. Then, every once in a while, look to your right or left—and if somebody's running with you, grab her and run together.

No Better Boss

Work is a good thing, even if it is messed up by the Fall. It's what we're supposed to do with much of our time in this life. So if you're not happy in your work, we hope you will find your way to something better and will remain faithful to your job responsibilities until you get there. We hope you'll work hard and bring all your God-given talents to bear on your goals. We hope you'll find a specific calling in life to go with your general calling to follow Jesus. (More on that coming up in chapter 11.) We hope you have a mate, or can find one, who will come alongside to encourage you and help you in fulfilling your calling.

Most of all, though, we hope you are serving the Lord and not your earthly boss. Trust in Him and look to Him to direct you into what He wants you to accomplish with your gifting, your time, and your energy. If you do that, it's a win no matter what anybody else might say.

And now we've come to an area of our lives that we'd rather not have to deal with—the battle to live holy. So many of us have failed in this area so many times that we may prefer to not even think about it. But that's why it's so important that we do. You see, you can have a win on the inside, just as you can in the outer parts of your life, such as your family and your work.

Our obedience matters to God because it shows we love Him. And we can make real progress toward holiness and purity through the same principles of authentic success that we've seen work in other areas of a man's life: trusting and serving God.

The Voice of Temptation

*When we're feeling a pull toward sin,
we can turn to Jesus and He will help.*

Because [Jesus] himself has suffered when
tempted, he is able to help those who are
being tempted.

—HEBREWS 2:18, ESV

I (Matt) am one of the most wired, wound-up people on the face of the
earth. I have an internal motor that never quits. I'm tense all the time. If I'm
sitting down, my leg bounces.

During one of my procedures for cancer treatment, the doctors shot me up
with this stuff that was supposed to knock me out. At first they gave me five
milligrams—the normal dose for people my height and weight. I woke up in
the middle of the procedure and said, "Hey, am I supposed to be awake?" So
they upped the dose and carried on. I woke up a second time and said, "Hey, I
don't think I'm supposed to be awake yet, am I?" So they upped the dose again.
This went on several more times. They ended up giving me *fourteen* milligrams
of the stuff—nearly three times the normal amount.

After the procedure, the doctor looked at me in the bed and said, "What
do you do for a living, anyway?"

"I'm a pastor."

"Oh really." He raised his eyebrows. "The only other guy I've ever known who has come close to being given that much drugs to knock him out was an Olympic athlete."

A few years after my cancer, I had elective surgery for something else. It wasn't that important, but there was a lot of pain involved afterward. So the doctor gave me a bottle of Vicodin, a powerful but addictive painkiller. The morning after the procedure, I was in a lot of pain. I toughed it out during the day, but that night I took the Vicodin.

Wow! Every muscle in my body relaxed. I didn't even know that was possible, particularly for such a wired guy like me. Every care in the world disappeared. I slept better than I've slept in twenty-five years. I had never done drugs as a kid, so after taking the Vicodin I told myself, *I now know why people do drugs!* I got up the next day, felt the pain again, took the Vicodin again, and experienced the same effect.

> When every fiber of your being is crying out to go a harmful direction, what do you do?

When I got up the third day, my pain was gone. I didn't need to take any more Vicodin. But I was tempted— *deeply* tempted—to pick up that drug and take it again just for the feeling it produced.

By the grace of God, I walked into the bathroom, grabbed the bottle of Vicodin, emptied the contents, and flushed the toilet.

I'm not telling you this to pat myself on the back. I haven't always been that wise in the face of every temptation I've encountered. I tell the story because this is a question every man wrestles with. How does a man seek the real win in times of temptation?

When every fiber of your being is crying out to go a harmful direction, what do you do?

Don't trust in your willpower. Again, the answer is to trust in God. If you'll turn to Jesus, He has the power to help you say no to the temptation and avoid the sin. And that's always better than having to recover from the sin after giving in to it!

That's why in this chapter we want to help you put up a strong defense against temptation and win over this attack of your spiritual enemy. And to begin, we've got to understand temptation better.

Temptation Isn't Sin

Think about the last time you were tempted. Can you picture it? What happened in that moment? Redefining success means we trust and serve God at all times, including those moments when we're tempted to go the other way.

Rest assured, temptation happens to every man—it even happened to Jesus. It's that moment when you haven't yet sinned but you want to. Your mind or your flesh is so ready to grab hold of that thought or speak that word or grab that thing that's outside of God's best for you. It's that moment when you're tired and your wife is in bed or your roommate is in bed, and you are all alone at the computer screen. Temptation is the moment *before* you click on that website. Or it's when your wife says something to you that you consider disrespectful. You feel slighted and have a desire in your heart to withdraw from her or to verbally jab back. It's that moment *before* you do. Or it's when you're driving on the freeway and somebody cuts you off. You feel your blood pressure rise and an instant impulse to speed ahead of him and cut him off. It's that split second *before* your foot hits the accelerator. What do you do?

When I (Colt) think about temptation, I think about when I first started college at the University of Texas. I quickly found that a college quarterback tends to attract a certain amount of attention from members of the opposite sex—and so that sets up temptation. Some of the attention I received came from women I didn't even know. They made it clear to me that they'd be interested in crossing boundaries I had set when it came to physical relationships.

I was not perfect in this area, and I made my fair share of bad choices. But

I was determined to reserve the deepest level of physical intimacy for sharing with one woman only—my future wife, whoever she would be.

Another one of the temptations I faced right after landing on campus was whether to drink alcohol. I didn't drink at all in high school, and there were several strong reasons for me to continue with that practice at UT. For one, it was illegal because I wasn't yet twenty-one. For another, I was on scholarship and I could easily get booted off the team for bad behavior, not to mention getting kicked out of school. And for a third, I'd set a goal of someday being the Longhorn starting quarterback. That meant I needed to stay the course physically, mentally, and spiritually, and focus all my attention on my goal.

> I quickly found that a college quarterback tends to attract a certain amount of attention from members of the opposite sex.

Even though I didn't drink, I still went to my share of parties. I had a lot of good friends at the university, some of whom were Christians and some who weren't. For me, going to parties was all about spending time with my friends. Some sort of alcohol always flowed at these parties, and someone would inevitably offer me a drink, although after a while they learned what my decision was in that area. Most people respected me for it. Yet sometimes when a drink was being held out to me, those were very real moments of temptation.

Scripture explains the process of what happens to us in the moment of temptation in James 1:13–15:

> Let no one say when he is tempted, "I am being tempted by God," for God cannot be tempted with evil, and he himself tempts no one. But each person is tempted when he is lured and enticed by his own desire. Then desire when it has conceived gives birth to sin, and sin when it is fully grown brings forth death. (ESV)

According to the Bible, then, your temptation all starts in your heart. You want something outside of God's best for your life and think that thing will provide exactly what you need. It's bad for you or it doesn't belong to you, but you want it anyway. Temptation isn't sin in and of itself. Temptation turns into sin only when you go after what you wrongfully desire. Sin happens when you give in to the temptation or pursue the harmful goal. It's like the fleshly desire conceives. After it's conceived, it has a baby. Scripture says that baby is called *sin*. The bad thing about that little sin baby is that it doesn't just stay there. The Scripture says it grows up and becomes an adult. That adult has a name.

Death.

To repeat: temptation isn't the same thing as sin. That's an important distinction to make. There is a big difference between being tempted to sin and actually sinning. Space exists in that vital moment for the Holy Spirit to work. When I (Matt) was younger, I used to beat myself up because I didn't understand that principle. I would walk around feeling guilty because I didn't get that. I equated temptation and sin, and I loathed myself every time I was tempted.

But think of it this way. Maybe you see an attractive woman on the beach. Your desire to look at her isn't sin—it's actually normal. God designed men to be visually attracted to women. Just because your flesh wants to look at that woman doesn't mean you have lusted. The desire has not yet conceived. There's a difference between being tempted to lust and letting that desire grow into sin.

I've talked with guys who, when tempted, have learned to respond well. They avert their eyes, hearts, and minds from the temptation and honor the Lord in the moment. But they still feel guilty because they *wanted* to progress down the path of sin. That was me when I was younger.

What I needed to hear then—and what you need to hear too—is that God does not get angry at you because you are tempted. You need to feel that and believe that and walk in that. If anything, what we're about to see is that, in a moment of temptation, God has sympathy for you. It's like Jesus says, "Yep, I can relate."

Now, if you see an attractive woman and are tempted to take a long second look *and you do,* that's sin. If, after the temptation comes, you undress her in your mind or if you imagine yourself physically being with her, then that's sin. What's happened at that moment is that temptation has conceived and given birth to sin. But again, temptation is not sin and we need to get to the place where we quit beating ourselves up because our flesh is tempted to act like flesh.

> Temptation isn't the same thing as sin. That's an important distinction to make.

Scripture undergirds this. First Corinthians 10:13 says, "No temptation has overtaken you that is not common to man" (ESV). That's comforting. A lot of times we suffer silently in our temptation, thinking, *I'm the only one on the planet who has ever been tempted to do that.* Or *I'm the only one on the planet who is struggling with this.* But the Bible is clear that experiencing the desires of the flesh is unbelievably common.

Do you know how freeing this is? For both men and women?!

If you are a wife and you are reading this book, let me be bold and say here that you shouldn't beat up your husband if he's being tempted. For example, if he's being tempted to take a long second look at another woman, that's not the same as lusting and it doesn't mean that he doesn't love you wholeheartedly. So, rather than beating him up, work to develop with your husband the kind of relationship where you can share your deepest concerns and support each other through them.

It's not easy for a man to say to his wife, "Honey, I'm being tempted right now. Would you pray for me?" But, wife, don't allow your heart to be hurt if he says something like that to you. That is evidence that the Holy Spirit is at work in his life! Come alongside him, pray for him, and help him in his temptation. Expect him to do the same for you when you're being tempted.

Scripture mentions how Jesus Himself was tempted. And it's because of this we can trust that He's sympathetic toward us in our own struggles with temptation.

Jesus Understands the Struggle to Surrender

This is what we know of Jesus and temptation: He "gets it" completely. Hebrews 4:15 says,

> We do not have a high priest who is unable to sympathize with our
> weaknesses, but we have one who has been tempted in every way, just
> as we are—yet was without sin. (NIV)

Do you see that? Jesus sympathizes with weakness. Why? Because Jesus Christ was tempted in "every way, just as we are," and yet He didn't sin, which is why we are to look to Him in those moments of temptation.

It's hard to fully understand what it means that Jesus was tempted in every way, but imagine what it might have meant. Maybe we think that Jesus was tempted only one time, perhaps when He was five years old. He was tempted to put his hand in the cookie jar but didn't. Then the rest of His life, through His teenage years, twenties, and thirties, He never struggled with anything again.

Nope.

We don't know the specific height and breadth and width of Jesus's temptations other than they were significant. Another passage in the book of Hebrews says,

> He [Jesus] had to be made like his brothers in every respect, so that
> he might become a merciful and faithful high priest in the service of
> God, to make propitiation for the sins of the people. For because he
> himself has suffered when tempted, he is able to help those who are
> being tempted. (2:17–18, ESV)

Note the word *suffered*, as in Jesus "suffered when tempted." It means it's possible that Jesus was tempted to steal when His father Joseph died and Jesus needed to take care of His mother, Mary, who wasn't rich.

It's possible Jesus was tempted to covet when He walked into Zacchaeus's house and saw all the earthly wealth and privilege that Zacchaeus owned.

It's likely Jesus was tempted to lust. He was good friends with two single women, Mary and Martha, and often spent time with them. Another time, another woman named Mary broke a jar of expensive perfume, poured it on Jesus's feet, and wiped His feet with her hair. Jesus might have been *tempted* then.

It's possible Jesus was tempted to pout with self-pity when He found His best friends asleep on the ground in the moment of the greatest need in His life, just before He was crucified.

It's possible Jesus was tempted to gloat over His accusers because they couldn't answer His questions, or was tempted to lash out with unrighteous anger at God.

You might think, *How in the world could Jesus be tempted with earthly wealth and privilege when He spent eternity in heaven?* The answer is because He wore human flesh. He literally walked in it. But there is one difference between Him and us. Jesus never sinned. That's why He is the one we turn to in the moments when we are tempted to turn toward the desires of our flesh.

> He is able to help those who are being tempted.
>
> —HEBREWS 2:18, ESV

There is one more amazing part of Hebrews 2:18. "He is able to help those who are being tempted" (ESV).

Let's say you are tempted today to say a white lie. Your flesh will desire to lie. You'll want to make yourself sound better than you should, or you'll want to get out of something you did or didn't do. You'll fight that temptation; in a sense, you'll "suffer" under it. Sometimes you'll resist the temptation, but other times you'll give in to it, and the temptation will conceive into sin. In that moment when temptation conceives into sin, the weight and the pressure and the suffering of temptation is alleviated. It's replaced by the suffering sin brings, but the suffering of temptation itself is alleviated in that moment.

Jesus never in His thirty-three years experienced the alleviation of temptation in His life. Never. Satan was constantly trying to get Jesus to sin, and our
Lord and Savior experienced a weight and a depth of temptation I don't think
you and I can possibly ever imagine. So as a result of what He walked through
and what He endured, what Jesus feels for you in the moment when you walk
through temptation is sympathy.

Do you see how freeing that fact is? Jesus is not up in heaven looking at you
in the moments when you feel weak and feeling disgust for you. He is not roll-
ing His eyes at you. And He's not inviting you to surrender because He wants
to make life *bad* for you. Scripture says that what Jesus Christ feels for you in
the moment when you are in the throes of temptation is sympathy. Jesus Christ
understands because He has shared the experience. He can come alongside you
and suffer with you in those moments.

That kind of identification is a tremendously powerful thing. As a pastor, I
(Matt) often have the opportunity to counsel people. Imagine a young couple
comes into my office, and the woman tells me she has recently had a miscarriage. There is only so much I can do to help and comfort, because I've never
had a miscarriage. I can intellectually understand what the couple is going
through, empathize with them, and pray with them. But I can't really get alongside them and feel the weight of their suffering because I have never gone
through that experience. I can't truly understand what they are walking in.

But if a person walks into my office and tells me he has cancer, it's a totally
different story. I understand that completely. I can come beside that person and
suffer with him. I understand his fears and concerns. I know firsthand what it's
like to worry that your children will grow up without a father. I can directly
relate to the indignity of having my body stuck and prodded with innumerable
needles and tests and medical procedures. I can relate firsthand to the worry
and uncertainty a life-threatening disease brings. I know all that because I've
been there.

The same is true of Jesus when it comes to understanding your temptation
and your struggle to surrender.

That's what Jesus Christ offers you—sympathy to suffer with every single moment in your life when your flesh desires to sin. Whatever you're being tempted to do, whatever suffering you're enduring, Jesus has been there too.

OUR PART

Jesus suffered when He was tempted, and because of that He is able to help us when we're tempted. That's really good news. He is able to come to our aid when we are in that moment of temptation—when our flesh has a desire to go a harmful direction but the desire has not yet conceived into sin.

> Do you want to overcome temptation? There's God's part and our part.

Do you want to overcome temptation? There's God's part and our part. He's responsible for understanding us and giving us the ultimate power to win. Our part is responding to His leadership in obedience.

The ways we can turn to Jesus for help in time of temptation include taking the following four actions.

1. Use the Word of God.

This sounds basic, almost something too simple to try. But how many of us have actually tried this in moments of temptation? It's the example that Jesus showed when He was tempted.

Early on in Jesus's ministry, the Spirit of God led Him out into the desert, where Satan approached Jesus and offered Him a temptation to take the easy way out. Satan took Jesus to the pinnacle of a high mountain, showed Him all the kingdoms and peoples of the world, and said, "I'll tell You what, Jesus. I'll give it all to You. You came to save these people anyway. Just bow down and worship me. You don't need to be crucified on a cross, become sin for all mankind, or be separated from Your Father. I'll just give them to You right now, okay? All You gotta do is worship me."

Jesus didn't want to go to the cross. That fact came out later in His prayers in the Garden of Gethsemane, as we will soon see. So it was a huge temptation for Him to be handed the kingdoms of the world. But at that precise moment, what did Jesus do?

He spoke Scripture that He had already read and memorized.

"Satan," Jesus said, "it is written that I shall worship the Lord God and worship Him alone." (See Matthew 4:10; Luke 4:8.)

Then Satan took off.

The Word of God is such a powerful tool in the moment of temptation. Your flesh wants what is a lie. But when you speak Scripture, you speak truth. The truth overcomes the lie. It sets the lie in perspective. Quoting God's Word, either from memory or by reading it straight from the Bible, is one of the most powerful tools we have in combating temptation.

A friend of mine, Halim Suh, realized the importance of Scripture in his everyday life as a hedge against temptation and sin. He began a daily Bible reading plan in which he would take one verse, or a section of verses, and read it, pray it back to God, and write down his thoughts about what he thought God was saying and how he could apply it to his life. He made a commitment to do this every day for a year. At the end of the year, he printed out his studies, bound them, and gave them to his children as a present.

This was a few years ago. To this day, Halim talks about how this "year in the Word" was one of the most spiritually fruitful years of his life.

2. Talk to God about your temptation.

Again, this sounds so simple. Pray. But how often do you actually pray when temptation hits you?

Think about Jesus. What did He do in the Garden of Gethsemane when He was only a few hours away from being tortured and crucified on the cross?

He prayed.

What was even worse than being crucified was that Jesus was actually about to become sin for us (2 Corinthians 5:21). Think about it. Jesus had never sinned. He had never known the sting and shame of sin. In the garden, Jesus is moments away from being separated from His Father, whom He has been with for all eternity, and actually *becoming* sin on our behalf. We know scripturally that in this moment, as Jesus is in the Garden of Gethsemane, He is in the midst of the greatest temptation of His life. He's actually on the ground, sweating blood. The temptation for Jesus is to not go through with the cross, find another way, and take the easy way out.

Watch the action. Matthew 26:36–40 says,

> Jesus came with them [His disciples] to a place called Gethsemane, and said to His disciples, "Sit here while I go over there and pray." And He took with Him Peter and the two sons of Zebedee [that's James and John], and began to be grieved and distressed. Then He said to them, "My soul is deeply grieved, to the point of death; remain here and keep watch with Me."
>
> And He went a little beyond them, and fell on His face and prayed, saying, "My Father, if it is possible, let this cup pass from Me; yet not as I will, but as You will." And He came to the disciples and found them sleeping, and said to Peter, "So, you men could not keep watch with Me for one hour?" (NASB)

Watch what He says. "Keep watching and praying" (verse 41, NASB). Jesus looks at His guys. They're asleep. He wakes them up, and He says, "Here is what you need to do. You need to keep watch and you need to pray." Why do you pray? Right here Jesus tells us "that you may not enter into temptation; the spirit is willing, but the flesh is weak."

You want to combat the weakness of your flesh?

Pray.

Jesus is in the greatest moment of temptation in His life, and He prays. He gets on His face, and He gets real about it, and He prays.

Likewise, the disciples are literally about to walk to the greatest temptation in their lives. Peter is a short time away from lopping some dude's ear off and denying Christ three times. Jesus looks at Peter and says, "Peter, you know what you need to be doing right now? You need to be praying because your spirit wants to do what's right, but buddy, your flesh is weak. So you need to pray."

> You want to combat the weakness of your flesh? Pray.

It's no different for you. Your spirit is willing, but your flesh is weak. The next time temptation hits you, in that moment when your flesh wants to do something that's outside of God's best, speak the truth of the Word of God into that moment. Then get on your face and pray.

When you're in front of the computer, and the temptation to look at pornography is coming at you like a lightning bolt, get on your face and say, "Jesus, I need Your strength right now."

When you realize how easy it would be to leave some earnings off your income tax return, or take a deduction you don't qualify for, pray about that. Pray hard.

When you get a flirtatious text from an attractive female coworker, and you start imagining how far you might be able to take it if you texted her back the same way, pray, pray, pray.

Say in prayer, "Jesus, I need You right here to help me right now. My spirit wants to do what's right, but my flesh is weak. I need Your strength." You will be shocked at the power that comes flooding over your life.

3. Love God.

Use the Word. Pray. And now love God. Again, simple. But one of the biggest tools to combat temptation is the practice of loving God.

In John 14:15 Jesus says, "If you love Me, you will keep My commandments" (NASB). Now, we have a problem with that verse. When we read that verse, we like to spin it. We like to look at that verse in a negative light, kind of like an "If…then" statement. Like, "Well, *if* you really loved Me, *then* you'd keep My commandments." But that's not at all what Jesus is saying.

The word *love* used in this verse is the Greek word *agapao.* It means "to choose to love," or "to pursue love." Jesus is saying something so cool and so simple, and it takes the pressure off of us. He's saying, "Hey, if you'll just choose to love Me, then the overflow of you loving Me is that you'll keep My commandments."

In other words, Jesus is saying you should focus on raising your affections for Him. When you do that, your affections for the world will dwindle. Let the temperature of your affections be raised for Him, and the temperature of your affections for the world will grow cold.

When I (Matt) am participating in an interview with someone we're thinking about adding to our staff at Austin Stone, I let the others ask the detailed questions. I ask the candidate only one question. I ask him or her, "When was the last time the thought of the gospel made you weep?" (What would your answer be?) If the person we're interviewing can't answer that question, I simply won't hire him or her. Why? Because I've realized there is a direct connection between a person's love for Jesus and that person's obedience to Him.

4. Stay in your lane.

How do you resist temptation? We've seen three other strategies, and here's one more.

Stay the course, and don't give yourself too many options.

When you run an offense in the NFL, you have hundreds of plays in your system, but I (Colt) think the ones that work the best are the ones with fewer options. Some plays have three to four different reads based upon coverage or blitzes. But there are also some that have one or two different reads that seem to always work. No matter what the defense does, I know that these plays have a chance. Having fewer options eliminates the thought process and allows me to just be in rhythm and make the throw.

This principle has good spiritual applications. Do we want a strong walk with God? Then we should keep it simple. If we worry about outside factors all the time, we are eventually going to make a mistake and fall out of our lane. Our focus should be completely on staying the course—that's the option that consistently leads to the true win. Hebrews 12:1 says, "Let us throw off everything that hinders and the sin that so easily entangles, and let us run with perseverance the race marked out for us" (NIV).

What might that look like?

- Decide once and for all to take your family to church each week. That way it's not an option to make a decision about every Saturday night or Sunday morning. It's just something you do.

- Decide once and for all that you won't watch things you shouldn't. Eliminate that option from your life. That way when you're ordering a movie or sitting in front of the television or computer, you'll be quicker to pass by the films you know won't be beneficial.

- Decide once and for all to be a man of integrity. If options come up to take the easy way out—a way that's morally wrong—the decision will be clearer for you. You know there are certain things you always or never will do. You won't sell your integrity for any price.

A Choice Every Day

One final thought. Hebrews 10:35–36 says,

> Do not throw away your confidence; it will be richly rewarded. You need to persevere so that when you have done the will of God, you will receive what he has promised. (NIV)

Perseverance is a commitment to be faithful, and it's a choice we don't simply make once and forget about. We make it every day. Sometimes *every minute* of every day.

Yes, it requires perseverance to overcome temptation. Jesus understands this. The real win means continually doing the will of God. It means doing it again and again and again and again, even when it's hard or burdensome to do it. When we persevere, we will receive what God has promised. In some way we'll be richly rewarded. Sure, every day we'll face temptation. But the key always is to turn toward Christ, not away from Him. The confidence is ours that He hears, listens, understands, and helps.

You can do this, even though temptation can prove to be a complex thing. Sometimes temptation is simple and blatant—like the junk that's prone to pass before our eyes. But sometimes the issue of temptation is much more encompassing. It involves a way we see the world and a big question of who we ultimately follow: ourselves or Christ.

> Do not throw away your confidence; it will be richly rewarded.
>
> — HEBREWS 10:35

First Corinthians 10:13 guarantees that there's no excuse when we give in to temptation. Jesus's help is enough. But you know and we know that sometimes we are going to give in. We're going to sin. Does this have to derail us from our quest for authentic success as men? If you don't know the answer to that, you soon will.

The Welcoming Arms of God

*When you fail morally (and you will),
and you then repent, God has
mercy and grace for you.*

Let us draw near with confidence to the
throne of grace, so that we may receive mercy
and find grace to help in time of need.

—HEBREWS 4:16, NASB

In the last chapter, I (Matt) told you how I managed to stop myself before
I gave in to the lure of using Vicodin just because it made me feel good. But I
don't want you to think I'm claiming to be a moral paragon—or that Colt is,
for that matter. We've made our share of mistakes.

I started walking closely with Jesus at the end of my first semester of college, and God brought a ton of healing in my life. I walked strong in the battle
against lust until the mid-1990s, when the Internet came on big. The Internet
is like having a *Playboy* magazine sitting on your desk twenty-four hours a day,
seven days a week. The invention of the smartphone has had the same result,
except now we're carrying the temptation around in our front pockets. Yes, I
was a Christian and was already thinking ahead toward a life of ministry. Yet
for a period I failed in this area of pornography, as so many men do.

I know you can relate. If porn isn't a problem for you, substitute anger. Pride. Selfishness. Gluttony. Laziness. Or whatever shows up in your sin profile.

It's so much better if we do what we learned in the preceding chapter—turn to Jesus for help in avoiding temptation. But when we don't, what then?

What do we do when we have fallen short of God's high moral standards for us? And what can we expect His reaction to be?

> Winning God's way does not have to be over for us when we've made a mistake.

Winning God's way does not have to be over for us when we've made a mistake. If we're trusting in Him, God has a way of welcoming us back from our detour and putting us back on the path to living in a way that fulfills His beautiful plan. As we'll see, if we're expecting Him to treat us like a coach chewing out his team that's trailing at halftime, we're wrong. He doesn't want to dress us down, shame us, or put us on the bench. He's got grace and mercy waiting for us the minute we return to Him.

The starting point for understanding all this better is getting underneath the surface problem of our sin.

THE ROOT CAUSE

If a man rejects God as the source of comfort, approval, security, or happiness, and if he tries to meet that need with something or somebody else, it becomes sin. The sin is harmful in and of itself, but the sin is only a surface issue. Beneath the surface is a deeper root issue.

Think of it this way. If you go out tonight with some friends, cross the line, drink too much, and get drunk, the drunkenness itself is wrong. You're being controlled by something other than the Spirit of God, and God says that's not to be part of the life of a follower of Christ (Ephesians 5:18). Yet something else is going on that's deeper than the sin of drunkenness. Drunkenness is only a symptom of a deeper root issue in your life.

Rewind the tape of that night. At the beginning of that night, long before you were ever drunk, your flesh, mind, or heart had a desire. It might have been the comfort the alcohol brought you in the form of escapism. It might have been the approval of your friends as you went out together. It might have been the false power brought about by booze. It might have been the security that came from having something else control you.

No matter what the root cause of the night's actions was, your flesh, mind, and heart worked in conjunction with your desire. Instead of satisfying that desire ultimately in the Lord, that root need set you on a course toward the sin of drunkenness.

So, to combat that drunkenness, it's one thing to work on the surface sin. But it's another thing entirely—a much more effective thing, actually—to dig underground and work on the root of the problem.

Consider another example. Let's say you go to work tomorrow and struggle with patience and kindness toward the guy next to you. He shirks his work, plays fantasy football on his computer all day, and then blames you when your team projects aren't completed on time. Then, even though this moocher is a moron, one day he gets a big, fat promotion—he becomes your direct supervisor. What then? How are you going to feel in that moment? You're going to be tempted to hate him, right?

Addressing the hate is one thing. But, again, that's the surface problem. Scripture indicates that any hatred you feel is actually a symptom of a deeper root issue. Your flesh, mind, or heart had a need that set you on a course toward hating your coworker. Maybe it was the approval of your boss or the security of knowing your coworkers thought you were great. Instead of having that need satisfied by God, your desires enticed you and carried you away from contentment in the Lord. You turned to the sin of hating your moronic coworker. (See James 1:14.)

Right about now, you're probably asking yourself how this process of digging under the surface to get to the root cause works. Okay, let's work through this together.

How to Get to the Root Cause

Start with this. Ask yourself a basic question: *Where do I sin?* In other words, pinpoint the surface problem. Where do you usually fall short of the glory of God?

People typically sin in one of two areas. First, there's the external stuff that's easier to spot. Things like anger, sexual immorality, addictions, workaholism, gossip, compromise in business, and lying. Then there's the internal stuff. Internal sins are harder to spot because you can hide them from people more easily—things like fear, resentment, not forgiving people, self-righteousness, and bitterness.

So the first part of the process involves figuring out where your sin lies. What are you turning to in order to satisfy yourself?

> Ask yourself a second question: Why do I struggle with this surface sin?

Got that in mind? It might take awhile of doing some soul searching. You might want to get a journal and a pen and write some stuff down. Or maybe you want to work through this chapter with the help of a trusted friend or men's group.

Then, once you've got the surface problem in mind, go deeper. Ask yourself a second question: *Why do I struggle with this surface sin?*

Have you ever thought about that? It's actually a really profound question. *Why? What is the desire I have in my heart that carries me away to that sin? What is the need I'm trying to fulfill by turning to this sin?*

A couple of years ago I (Matt) went through this process of going deeper with the problem I already confessed to you: pornography.

Back when that was a problem for me, I began to ask the question, *Why is this a temptation for me? What is the root need I have in my heart that is causing me to have this desire to look at something I know is sinful, destructive, and ultimately ridiculous?*

It wasn't a straightforward answer at first. I loved Jesus Christ and was deeply committed to following Him. I loved my wife and was (and still am) deeply attracted to her. Our intimacy is healthy. So I kept puzzling over the questions: *Why in the world is this a temptation for me? What is the need I'm trying to fulfill?*

For the life of me, I couldn't figure it out. So I did something I encourage you to do. I went into my bedroom, closed the door, and said to myself, "I'm not coming out of here until I get to the bottom of this."

It took about an hour for me to process what my root need was, the area down deep that I was trying to fulfill. And here's what I came up with. Every time I'm tempted in this area, it's because I am trying to satisfy a desire for approval.

Approval—that was the root cause of my temptation.

See, when I was growing up, I longed for my dad's approval, but he was not always the best at conveying that. These days, my dad and I have a great relationship, and he speaks a ton of value into my life. But back then he was one of those dads who would often focus on the negative aspects of my character instead of praising me for the positive. For instance, I'd be playing baseball in Little League and would get three hits and strike out once. Hitting a baseball three out of four times is really good, and if you carried out that average all the way through the major leagues, you'd be in the Hall of Fame. But my dad was the kind of guy who'd always ignore the three hits and ask about the one strikeout instead. Anybody else have a dad like that?

The lack of approval from my dad showed up in different ways. My dad was a fireman, so he was comfortable working with his hands. On his days off, he'd build and fix stuff. But I'm mechanically inept and can't build or fix anything. I'd rather read or play football—I'm kind of a bookworm-slash-jock. So he'd come to me and say, "Hey, let's go work on the car," and I'd tell him I didn't want to. I could tell it disappointed him. So those exchanges between us produced in me this longing for his value and his approval.

And it wasn't just my dad.

My mom and I had a great relationship. She's passed away now, but she was my best friend in a lot of ways before she died. Yet she said something to me one time that cut deep, and I'd never quite been able to forget it.

It was just the second or third time I'd ever preached. I was twenty-two and my mom was there. I was intimidated, nervous, and insecure. (Still am when it comes to preaching, in a lot of ways.) At the end of the sermon, she walked up to me and gave me a little hug. Of course I wondered what she thought.

> My dad was a fireman, so he was comfortable working with his hands.

Now, we had a pastor my mom and I both really liked—Chris Osborne. He was an unbelievable preacher and a godly man all around. So I preached this message and felt like it went well, and then my mom came up to me and I asked, "Mom, how did it go?"

And she said, "Well, Matt, it was good, but you're no Chris Osborne."

I know she was just kidding, but that one line stuck with me. My preaching was good, but… There was always a *but*. Have you ever felt that way?

From the time I was a little kid, I desperately wanted the people I loved to speak value and approval into my life. I longed for them to say, "Matt, I see that God has His hand on you. I like you. I like what God is doing in your life." But that approval was missing.

Fast-forward a bunch of years. When I was sitting there in my bedroom, trying to figure out why sexual sin had been such a problem for me in high school and was now a temptation for me as an adult, it hit me like a ton of bricks. The falsely aggressive nature of the women in those situations appealed to my flesh. They were taking the lead relationally, so to speak, and the idea of women doing that with me provided me with a false, weird, stupid, and sinful sense of approval.

It was a massive moment of victory in my life to realize that the desire for approval had the capacity to carry me away to sin. I began to pray through that and open my heart to Christ in this area. These days, whenever I begin to feel temptation, I recognize it as the longing for approval and remember, *Hey, I've failed enough to know there is nothing in this world that can satisfy that desire of my heart except Christ.*

In that moment of temptation, I do what the Scripture says. I take that desire and run to God. Jesus reminds me that because of the work He did on the cross, there is no barrier between God and man anymore. God approves of me greatly. He loves me unreservedly.

When you get to the root cause of your sin—whatever it is—you'll be at the same point of being able to see that it can never satisfy you like Jesus can.

Don't Deny; Instead Satisfy

Usually, we men are told to *deny* ourselves in our time of need. Just man up and pull ourselves up by our bootstraps—that's what we're told.

But the Bible indicates the opposite. The key, actually, is to *satisfy* ourselves. Don't look at the desires of your heart, flesh, and mind and stuff them down or pretend like they don't exist. But take those desires and satisfy them deeply, not in the garbage, but at the throne of Jesus Christ.

Satisfy yourself.

Not in the junk of the world, but in Jesus.

"How do you actually do that?" you might ask. It's really pretty simple. If God has "put eternity into man's heart" (Ecclesiastes 3:11, ESV), as we looked at in chapter 2, then on a daily basis we should look to the eternal to fill those desires. On any given day you are going to go after and pursue things that are of the world and cannot satisfy. Or you are going to pursue eternal things that do. It's that straightforward.

A friend of mine once explained to me that every action we take within a given day has one of three effects on our souls. Some actions are neutral. Some actions push our hearts further away from the Lord. Still other actions draw us nearer to God and satisfy those eternal longings that God has placed in the heart of every man.

He told me that he tries to take time each day to do things that satisfy the eternal longing of his heart. For my friend, worship music is something that draws his heart near to the Lord. On his commute home from work, he often turns off the sports talk radio and listens to a few worship songs. That time of worship really fills his heart, rights his spirit, and connects him with the Lord.

The Christian life is less about denying the bad things that hurt us and more about satisfying the true longings of our souls with good things that fulfill us. And the good things that fill us are two amazing qualities that God holds out to us.

Traffic Tickets and Cheeseburgers

You might think of the two strongest words in the Bible as *power* and *wrath*. Or maybe *heaven* and *hell*. But Hebrews 4:15–16, a passage we looked at briefly already in chapter 8, points to a different pair of words. Let's look at it more closely now.

> We do not have a high priest who cannot sympathize with our weak-
> nesses, but One who has been tempted in all things as we are, yet
> without sin. Therefore let us draw near with confidence to the throne
> of grace, so that we may receive mercy and find grace to help in time
> of need. (NASB)

Do you see the huge promise in this passage? If we draw near to Jesus, He gives us two things in our moment of need. Those are the two most powerful words in the Bible:

- mercy
- grace

They're immensely powerful, because mercy and grace will satisfy the part of us that was causing us to need something in the first place.

What exactly do the mercy and grace of Jesus look like? What are these things He gives us that can satisfy the longings of our hearts? *Mercy* and *grace* are some of the words that can get jumbled up in our heads a lot of times. We don't know what they mean, even though we hear or say them our whole lives.

Here's how I (Colt) believe the Bible defines those two words. One word sounds like a negative, and the other sounds like a positive. But really, both are very, very good.

Mercy *is when God doesn't give you a punishment you deserve.*

Grace *is when God gives you a blessing you don't deserve.*

See the difference?

A good example of mercy is that you got hungry for a cheeseburger, set down this book, and went for a drive to your nearest hamburger joint. You were really hungry, so in a rush to taste that burger you were speeding along at eighty miles per hour in a sixty-mile-per-hour zone. An officer pulled you over. He came over to your side window, his ticket book in hand, and said, "Hey, you were speeding. Did you know that?"

And you were like, "Yeah, I did. But I couldn't wait to taste that double-double with extra onions."

But then something funny happened. He put his ticket book in his back pocket and said, "Tell you what I'm going to do. I can appreciate a good cheeseburger as much as the next man, so I'm not going to give you a ticket. I'm going to give you a warning."

What is he showing you in that moment?

Mercy.

He did not give you a punishment you deserved.

Okay, same scenario, but with a different result this time. In your rush to the burger joint you're pulled over, but this time the officer says, "All right, here's the deal. The ticket for going twenty miles per hour over the limit costs $345 in this state. You deserve that ticket, but here's what I'm going to do." He pulls out his wallet and places the exact amount of money—$345—into your hand. "I'm going to pay your ticket for you," he says. "And not only that, but I'm going to give you a police escort all the way to the hamburger stand. Let's go."

> Grace.
> He's giving you a blessing you don't deserve.

What's he showing you then?

Grace.

He's giving you a blessing you don't deserve.

How do you feel when somebody shows you mercy or grace? Pretty grateful, right? You feel like it just made your day. With mercy and grace, your life just got good.

Ephesians 2:1–3 talks about what we deserve, and it's not good.

> You were dead in your trespasses and sins, in which you formerly walked according to the course of this world, according to the prince of the power of the air [Satan], of the spirit that is now working in the sons of disobedience. Among them we too all formerly lived in the lusts of our flesh, indulging the desires of the flesh and of the mind, and were by nature children of wrath, even as the rest. (NASB)

That means we all once deserved wrath. We deserved separation from an all-holy God. Once, we were dead in our trespasses and sins. We were as dead as a corpse, spiritually speaking, and we walked according to the course of this world. We indulged the desires of our flesh, and by our nature, we were children of wrath.

But Ephesians 2:4–5 has a pretty cool follow-up to that. This is where it gets really good.

God, being rich in mercy, because of His great love with which He loved us, even when we were dead in our transgressions, made us alive together with Christ. (NASB)

That's mercy. God did not give us what we deserved. But that's not all. James 4:1–8 talks about the passions that are at war within us. We desire things, so we quarrel and covet to get them. Then James shows the solution. It's offered to us, simply and boldly.

But he gives more grace. (James 4:6, ESV)

Not only does Scripture tell us that the grace of God is enough for us during our moments of temptation and sin, but the unmerited favor of God is also a way that God shows His love for us. You see, God not only saved us from our sin, but as Romans 8:15 tells us, He didn't stop there. He adopted us as His sons! In light of this, we can view God not only as our Savior, but as our Dad. That's not just a gift of grace, but that is a gift of amazing grace!

For all you fathers out there, think about it in this way. How much of a joy is it for you to give good gifts to your children? It's amazing to see the looks on their faces when they realize their dad didn't only think of them but went a step further to give them a desire of their hearts. If earthly dads get joy from giving good gifts to their children, how much more do you think our heavenly Father enjoys giving good gifts to us (see Matthew 7:11)?

James 1:17 says, "Every good gift and every perfect gift is from above, coming down from the Father" (ESV).

THE BIG DEER

I (Colt) want to tell you a story about a unique gift my heavenly Father gave me. To this day, I believe with all my heart it was a gift of God's grace. Now, if you grew up in the city, this story may not make much sense to you. But if you're a country boy, it will make all the sense in the world.

As we said earlier in the book, in my junior year at UT, we lost a crucial game to Texas Tech in the last seconds of the fourth quarter. As bad as that loss was, the consequence was even more difficult to swallow. Earlier in the year we had beaten Oklahoma pretty handily. But because of the way the BCS rules were laid out, since we lost to Tech, we were not allowed to play in the Big 12 Championship game, and Oklahoma took our place as representative from the Big 12 South. They played against Missouri, whom we had also beaten handily earlier in the year. Honestly, days after our loss to Tech, I was still too depressed even to watch Oklahoma and Missouri play in the Big 12 Championship. So I did what all good country boys do when life gets disappointing.

> I did what all good country boys do when life gets disappointing. I went hunting.

I went hunting.

While the rest of the country was watching football, there I was, pretty down on myself and sitting on the side of a hill in the freezing cold. Alone with my thoughts, I started to pray. I poured my heart out to the Lord and confessed to Him that I didn't understand all of His ways but that I trusted Him. Then all of a sudden I had an idea. With a smile coming across my face, I asked my heavenly Father a question. I said, "Lord, we didn't win the big game that would have sent us to the Big 12 Championship, but today, would You let me see a big deer?"

True story—not long after that, the biggest deer I had ever seen up to that point came walking out. Now, years later, he still looks pretty awesome hanging on my wall.

Having said all that, let me put a question out there. Does God always bless us this way when we ask?

No. As we'll be learning in more detail in the next chapter, God uses disappointment, failure, and suffering to draw us near to Him and teach us faithfulness in ways that success simply can't.

But do I believe that in that moment my heavenly Father was giving me a good gift?

The answer is yes. Not only did He save me from my sin, not only did He adopt me into His family, but if those things were not enough, He lifted my chin up by blessing my socks off one cold December morning.

It's called grace.

Play in Your World, with God's Help

In my (Colt's) world of professional football, *mercy* and *grace* aren't words that are used very much. If I throw an interception, the other team doesn't hand the ball back to me on a platter. They take it and run straight at me as hard as they can. Or if I have an average game, the media and the blogosphere aren't easy on me. They tell me in no uncertain terms what they think of my play.

No, professional football is all about the toughest, harshest kind of impartiality around. This game doesn't give you what you don't deserve; it only gives you what you do deserve—and sometimes not even that. Chances are, that might characterize the world you live in too.

I'm so thankful that mercy and grace are attributes of God. That's what's so amazing about Jesus, because I am definitely not perfect. I have my ups and downs. I make mistakes. But Jesus Christ is the only man who is perfect, and He invites me to win His way.

What the world signifies as success involves winning the Heisman, getting paid a lot of money, and playing in the NFL. But for me, I'm a success because I have Jesus Christ living inside me.

In my senior year of college, Matt and I talked about how the truth that Christ lives in me should impact my daily life. In Colossians 3:3 the apostle Paul wrote, "You have died, and your life is hidden with Christ in God" (ESV). Consider that for a minute. Our lives are hidden with Christ in God! Our identities are now wrapped up in the identity of the King of kings and the Lord of lords! So when I think about it that way, if my life is truly hidden in

Christ, I have nothing to win, nothing to lose, and nothing to prove. When we live in light of that truth, we are achieving the real win, the ultimate win.

Now, absolutely, I'm going to keep playing hard in the world God has called me to. I'm going to keep shooting for my earthly goals, as I believe God is calling me to play in the NFL and to play great.

> In my world of professional football, mercy and grace aren't words that are used very much.

But those earthly goals are not what define me—not ultimately, anyway. As I breathe my last breath, I'm going to come running home and stand face to face with Jesus. For the first time in my life, every single longing and every single desire of my heart will be completely satisfied in the face and name and person of Jesus Christ. I'll be completely satisfied, completely at peace. That's what I try to keep in mind every day.

In the meantime, Jesus gives me the confidence that when my life is based on Him, I'm standing on the Rock. My call is to come to Him every single day. I might not win every day in the eyes of the world, but Jesus promises grace and mercy every day to help me in my time of need.

With Jesus, I can have full confidence. That same promise is true for you too.

What's strange, and usually hard to accept, is the way God's grace and mercy appear mixed in with loss, disappointment, and pain. But coming to grips with God's sovereignty in our worst times is what's going to grow us into maturity as men of God and help to finish His work in our lives.

Hard School

*No one likes trials and suffering,
but God uses them to turn us
into the men He wants us to be.*

Consider it all joy, my brethren, when you
encounter various trials, knowing that the
testing of your faith produces endurance. And
let endurance have its perfect result, so that
you may be perfect and complete, lacking in
nothing.

—JAMES 1:2–4, NASB

Have you ever experienced a serious difficulty in your life? Maybe
you're going through a difficult time right now.

Perhaps your career has not advanced to the degree you thought it would
when you got out of college. Maybe your marriage has proved more difficult
than you expected, and you wonder if it's ever going to get better. Maybe, like
me (Matt), you've seen an illness come into your life that made you face your
own mortality.

Difficulties such as these often make us wonder where God is. Is there any greater purpose for the difficulty? Can God accomplish anything good through the hard time? Or are you experiencing this trial all for nothing?

Take heart in the promises of Scripture. As the verses quoted above say, we can actually welcome trials with joy if we recognize that they lead to endurance and that this endurance in its turn leads to spiritual maturity. In this way trials can actually contribute to our becoming "perfect and complete, lacking in nothing." That's a win for sure!

But there's more. Consider the verse that comes next: James 1:5.

If any of you lacks wisdom, let him ask of God, who gives to all gener-ously and without reproach, and it will be given to him. (NASB)

So we've got a promise of wisdom coming directly *after* James 1:2–4, which exhorts us to consider it a joy whenever we encounter trials. What's the point?

For the believer, trials produce wis-dom. And wisdom is more valuable than just about anything. Through wisdom we learn to be content with what God is doing in our lives, even if it isn't what we wanted, because we trust Him and His greater plans for us. He's got the real win; we don't. And if some suffering is the price we have to pay for it, we're ready to accept that and be glad.

> He's got the real win; we don't. And if some suffering is the price we have to pay for it, we're ready to accept that and be glad.

But knowing this truth and living by it are two different things. So let's take a closer look at the real win when it comes to dealing with life's difficulties.

Much More than a List

In chapter 4, I (Matt) told a story of how, after ten years of marriage, I had es-sentially lost the heart of my wife. She wasn't going to leave me, and we still loved each other, but because of my pursuit of my career, she felt disconnected and distant from me. It all came to a head one New Year's Eve a few years back. After a pretty severe argument between us, she took off to be with our friends, and I stayed at home. Both of us were at a place where we were emotionally spent and ready to give up.

That night after my wife had left, I lay in our bathtub, crying my eyes out. In desperation I cried out to the Lord, "God, I am so weary of this. If my marriage is ever going to change, *You* are going to have to do it. And, God, I want You to start by changing me. God, please change my heart and give me the wisdom to love my wife the way You have called me to love her."

Call that a moment of surrender. In that season of trial and desperation, something stirred in my heart as I cried out to God for wisdom. And God began to answer my prayer. He began to change me.

The next day, with a renewed strength, I began a journey to discover and apply what it looked like to be the husband I was called to be. I wanted to win back the heart of my wife. Through counsel, study of Scripture, and asking my wife a ton of questions about how to love her well, I made a list of things I wanted to implement in order to be the husband God was calling me to be.

1. I will tame my tongue. When it comes to my wife, I need to be quick to listen, slow to speak, and slow to anger.
2. I will talk to my wife the way I would if a special and important person were visiting my home.
3. I will always be upbeat and positive in my interactions with my wife. I am not called to critique her. I am called to love and accept her.
4. I won't use my words to try to *take* from her. I will just give and bless, thinking about what she needs, not what I need.
5. I will strive to serve my wife every day.
6. I will win my wife's heart so she, in turn, will *want* to be mine.
7. Just as divorce is not an option with me, I want that same reality to be true for negativity or harshness with my wife. It is *not* an option for me to be harsh with my wife. Not under any circumstance. Ever.

8. I will sow seeds of righteousness by consistently committing to walk with the Lord. God will give me the power to bear this fruit and love my wife wholeheartedly.

I wish I could tell you that I have implemented all the items on this list perfectly, but I haven't. Only one man will ever love my wife perfectly, and that is Jesus. Still, after a few years of practicing the wisdom I learned through my marital trials, I can say with confidence that God has done a miracle in my marriage. God has changed me, and as a result, our marriage has been healed. I have won the heart of my wife again, and we are more in love today than we were the day we married. I wish with all my heart that I could have learned these lessons without walking through all the junk. But it was through the trials that I learned wisdom. And you can too.

THE BEST THING YOU CAN ASK FOR

Redefining winning God's way means we trust and serve God at all times, and that means a man can experience unexpected benefits even when he goes through hard times. He transforms from being a spectator to being a participant in the lives of the people he cares for. He learns what's truly important in life. He lives with unction. Unfortunately, rarely can we learn these aspects of our character apart from trials and suffering.

Have you ever thought that a difficult situation can actually be a good thing? Have you ever thought about the solid biblical truth that God is using your trials to build you into the man He wants you to be? Plenty of folks don't believe that. They falsely believe that God is in the business of providing nothing but prosperity. When we truly trust God, they say, God always makes us happy, healthy, and wealthy. If you're suffering in any way, they continue to say, it's only because of a lack of faith.

It can be easy to fall into that trap. Like, if something bad is happening to you, it must mean that God doesn't love you. Or if you could just squeeze out some more faith, then all would be well.

But that's a lie from the pit of hell. Study the Bible, and you will soon find out what *isn't there*. What's missing from the Bible are stories about men who do everything right, never experience any hardships, and see God continually blessing them with easy lives. God never defines the greatness of man as "winning" in the sense of achieving the power, prestige, and prosperity that the world values. God always defines the greatness of a man as being faithful to God no matter what circumstance he finds himself in.

> He transforms from being spectator to being a participant in the lives of the people he cares for.

Over and over again in Scripture you see stories of men who walk through affliction, trial, failure, pain, and loss. Yet they do it by trusting God and walking in His faithfulness. That's the real win we're talking about here. And God looks at those people and says, "Well done." Unless you've walked through trials and have learned to trust God in the midst of those trials, it's hard to be truly effective as a man of God and a minister to others. The trials become part of God's perfect plan for your life.

That seems counterintuitive at first. But anyone can praise God when everything's going well. It's when men praise God in the difficult times that speaks the loudest. Ask yourself, who offers a bigger testimony to the world? Is it a man who holds up the Lombardi Trophy and says, "I give God the glory for this win"? Or is it a man who suffers much and says, "I give God the glory no matter what"?

As we've already discussed, I (Colt) know what it's like to go through challenges. For instance, I've gone through stretches where my team has lost games, and I hate that. But the down, stressed feeling involves more than not winning games. It's about figuring out what really matters in life.

True, losing games sometimes feels like the end of the world for me (as silly as that sounds). I put so much time and effort and energy into being the best quarterback I can be that I don't ever think I should fail. But it happens. And when it happens, I have got to be at peace in my heart to understand that God is in complete control no matter the circumstances we are dealt in life or in football. There is not one part of me that doesn't want to hold up a Super Bowl trophy someday. That is my biggest goal in football. And I believe it will happen one day. But if it never does, will that mean that my faith will waver because God didn't allow that to happen? Absolutely not!

The real win associated with going through difficulties involves more than being able to empathize and minister to others going through difficulty, although that's a part of it. Another benefit is that we begin to value what's truly important. We learn to trust God more.

I draw a lot of inspiration from the example of King Solomon in this area, particularly when he succeeded his father, David, as king. Not long after Solomon was crowned, God came to Solomon in a dream and said, "Ask what you wish Me to give you" (1 Kings 3:5, NASB).

Wow! Solomon could have asked for riches, power, success, happiness, security, wealth beyond imagination, good health—you name it! Can you imagine if God came to you and asked the same thing? What would you ask for? Right away, I'd sure be tempted to ask for a solid winning season and a Super Bowl ring. That's not wrong, but watch what Solomon asks for. Something way better! First Kings 3:8–9 records his answer to God:

> Your servant is in the midst of Your people which You have chosen, a
> great people who are too many to be numbered or counted. So give Your
> servant an understanding heart to judge Your people to discern between
> good and evil. For who is able to judge this great people of Yours? (NASB)

Not what you'd expect, is it? In verses 10–13, watch how God responds:

> It was pleasing in the sight of the Lord that Solomon had asked this
> thing. God said to him, "Because you have asked this thing and have
> not asked for yourself long life, nor have asked riches for yourself, nor

have you asked for the life of your enemies, but have asked for yourself discernment to understand justice, behold, I have done according to your words. Behold, I have given you a wise and discerning heart, so that there has been no one like you before you, nor shall one like you arise after you. I have also given you what you have not asked, both riches and honor, so that there will not be any among the kings like you all your days." (NASB)

How many people, if given the opportunity by God to ask for anything, would ask for wisdom? God not only gave Solomon wisdom, He gave him riches and honor on top of that. And if that were not enough, God said, "There will be not be any among the kings like you all your days" (verse 13, NASB).

The lessons to us in this are awesome. If you are going through a difficult time or if you've got a huge task in front of you as Solomon did, note that Solomon asked God for discernment to carry out his job as king, but he did not ask God to do the job for him. Solomon didn't ask God to lighten the load.

The same is true for us. The lesson is to ask God for wisdom to know what to do and courage to follow through. But don't ask God for ease. The trial might well be part of God's perfect plan for your life. James 1:5 promises that God will give wisdom to any who ask. It is not a wisdom isolated from trials and suffering. When you are in the dumps or are in a valley and can't seem to find your way to the top, wisdom is an important tool in continuing forward. When we ask God for wisdom, we are ultimately asking to be like Christ, for 1 Corinthians 1:24 identifies Christ as "the wisdom of God."

> When we ask God for wisdom, we are ultimately asking to be like Christ.

I realize that people have problems more difficult than mine, and I am blessed more than I deserve. As I walk through challenging stretches in my career, it would be easy to ask God for success, honor, Super Bowls, or whatever.

But what I see in the Scriptures is that God loves a man whose greatest desire is wisdom, discernment, and holiness. So, personally, I want to change course. I don't want to ask God to take me out of the valley and the tough times. I ask God to give me wisdom and discernment as I walk through them.

Wisdom doesn't mean being removed from difficulty. It's having the ability to do the right thing in the midst of wrong things going on around us. It's the ability to stand up and make a positive impact when negativity is all around. This is what God calls us to do. No matter how tough it gets, God wants us to go through our challenges for a greater purpose.

More than a Grasshopper

Take heart. If you're going through a difficult time right now, if you have a goal in front of you that you can't seem to achieve, if you've achieved a goal but it wasn't as satisfying as you'd hoped, or if there's a huge challenge in front of you that seems daunting, you're in good company. Many other men could say the same. I (Colt) certainly could.

Awhile back I was going through a rough stretch in my career. I'd just begun as starting quarterback in Cleveland, and the media constantly asked me what I needed to do to secure my spot as quarterback of the franchise. It was getting talked about every day in the news and the blogosphere. Everyone seemed to have a strong opinion. Then I got sidelined with a concussion and didn't know when I'd be back to play. Talk about adding stress on stress. I went through a solid week when all I wanted to do was sit on my couch and think. Every aspect of my life felt caught up in football.

During that time I did a lot of praying, Bible reading, and journaling. This is what I wrote in a journal.

Over the last sixteen months, my life has felt like everything but promising. It has been one struggle after struggle, one test after test. All the while, nothing seems to be getting any better. I pray to God daily, sometimes all day long, and hear no answers as to why the struggles continue. I seek God constantly, asking Him to help me through this. I knock on the door, and it just seems like I get no answers. My faith is being tested, because what I love to do (play football) has become miserable! The only time I have peace during my day is when I lay my head down and go to sleep. That is the only time I don't feel extreme amounts of pressure.

I will never give up on being the best quarterback I can be, and I know I will be there soon. But in order to get there, my attitude on all of this has to change. I realize that I've placed this game way higher on the totem pole than it should be. It has become my idol. It has become obvious to me that football can't fulfill all my needs and desires.

So what's the solution?

I must become lesser. And God must become greater!

During this difficult time, I drew a lot of encouragement from the story of Joshua and Caleb in Numbers 13.

As the Israelites neared the Promised Land, Moses sent twelve spies to look over the land and report what they found. When the spies came back, they said the land was amazing—it flowed with milk and honey, everything they'd ever want or need. But only two of the twelve, Joshua and Caleb, said that the Israelites were capable of conquering the land. The other ten reported that the people in the land were as strong and powerful as giants. They were like "grasshoppers" compared to the Canaanites, the ten spies said (Numbers 13:33), and they counseled the Israelites to stay where they were in the desert.

A similar question faced me. With the difficulties I was going through at my job, was I going to be like the ten scared spies or like the two bold ones? Caleb and Joshua had deep convictions about God's character. They knew that God had brought them out of slavery in Egypt and led them all the way through the desert. God wasn't going to allow them to be destroyed before they fulfilled the calling He had placed on their lives. Caleb and Joshua believed that somehow and some way God would deliver them. He was going to complete the good work He had started in their lives (Philippians 1:6).

That was the invitation God was holding out to me too—just like He holds out to you. If we want to really win, we need to believe as Joshua and Caleb believed. The difficulty in front of them seemed great, but they trusted God's leading. Faith is more about living with God than it is about getting something from God. When I trust in Him, I pursue Him more and I understand more of His character. He is always good, all the time. I certainly believe God has placed me in this position, and I am watching to see exactly how He handles it. God is watching me to see if I pursue Him or if I will sulk and feel sorry for myself.

> God is watching me to see if I pursue Him or if I will sulk and feel sorry for myself.

That's our call too. We have to step out and trust God! Each day we need to wake up and declare to ourselves that, no matter what, we need to trust God. If we want to see our faith grow, we have to come to conclusions about who God is. He is good, sovereign, trustworthy, and unchanging. And even when we can't see that clearly, we need to trust anyway. That means:

- Even when we feel like God is a million miles away from our situation, we will trust anyway.
- Even when we think we are fighting an uphill battle alone, we will trust anyway.
- Even when we feel that others are blessed tremendously more than we are, we will trust anyway.
- Even when we get jealous and mad, we will trust anyway.
- Even when we feel like God shows no favor toward us, we will trust anyway.
- Even when we strive to do everything the right way and honor Him, and it seems like our efforts are useless, we will trust anyway.

Yes, I strive to play great so that I can glorify God. I compete and train and work hard so that I will have the opportunity to honor God in front of millions. Does that mean God is going to guarantee that will happen? Absolutely not.

When I go through difficult times, does that mean I shouldn't have a determination to win when I play? No, I definitely should do that each time I compete. But just because I want to win at football, it doesn't mean that's what God needs. He has a plan, and I need to trust it. I have to display faith and trust and show obedience to the fact that I'm not in control; God is. How He wants to use me is totally up to Him.

WHEN GOD SEEMS FAR OFF

It was during a long season of difficulty in my life that I (Colt) made an observation that has changed everything with regard to how I look at the trials I am facing. I was reading Hebrews 11 about the great men of faith in Scripture, and I noticed something I had never seen before.

You see, the media and the world in general lift up men who win, that is, men who are successful in an outward sense, and say that those men are the "great" men of the world. But as I read Hebrews 11, something hit me like a lightning bolt. The Bible never tells a story of a man whose life was defined by ease and earthly success and calls him "great." There is not a single story of any guy who, because he lived well or had a desire to glorify God, was blessed with success upon success. It's simply not there.

There is in the Bible, however, story after story of great men of faith who walked through trials. Suffering, testing, pain. Not one great man in Scripture didn't have to endure many hardships. Not one. Think about the life stories of the great men in the Bible.

- *Abraham:* Called to leave his home. Challenged to put his son Isaac on the altar and put a knife to his throat.
- *Joseph:* Abandoned by his family. Sold into slavery by his brothers. Forced to live in a foreign land the majority of his life.
- *Moses:* Had to deal with the rejection of his people over and over again. Forced to live forty years in a desert, all because he was being obedient to God. Never entered the Promised Land.
- *Jeremiah:* Not one shred of success in more than seventy years of ministry. The crazy thing is that this was what God called him to do!

- *Paul:* Shipwrecked, abandoned, betrayed, gossiped about, tortured, beheaded.
- *Jesus:* Literally lived a perfect life, yet was misunderstood, tortured, abandoned, and crucified on the cross.

My point is that the world loves stories of men for whom it seems everything falls into place, the kind of stories in which everything seems to come easily and the results are win after win.

But the Bible shows stories about men who encountered difficulties, often failed, and suffered greatly. But they praised God anyway.

Here's the contrast: The world's definition of greatness equals success. But the Bible's definition of greatness equals faith in the midst of suffering.

Paul tells us in Romans that "we are more than conquerors" (8:37, ESV). I encourage you to be a conqueror and to be more than a grasshopper in every area of life—work, marriage, family. Be like Caleb and Joshua. Caleb said amid the crowd and all those who doubted, "We should go up and take possession of the land, for we can certainly do it" (Numbers 13:30, NIV).

> The world's definition of greatness equals success. But the Bible's definition of greatness equals faith in the midst of suffering.

Caleb and Joshua lived by faith. They felt the presence of God and trusted that no one was greater than the Lord. No one was stronger, no one more powerful—no one! And with Him, the Israelites could conquer anyone or anything. These two men put their complete trust in God, and that's how we should live!

What's the Secret?

In this area of enduring trials, as suffering shapes our lives over the long term, Philippians 4:11–13 points us to the true win. Paul says,

I have learned in whatever situation I am to be content. I know how to
be brought low, and I know how to abound. In any and every circumstance, I have learned the secret of facing plenty and hunger, abundance
and need. I can do all things through him who strengthens me. (ESV)

So what does being content mean? Our definition would probably lean
toward being settled, successful, comfortable, self-satisfied, happy with the way
we perform, and happy with whatever circumstances we face.

But in the Bible it means being sufficient in the Lord. We are able to say, "I
don't need anything else, because I have the Lord." And mean it.

Paul certainly went through hard times. In 2 Corinthians 11:23–27, he
wrote,

[I am a servant of Christ] with far greater labors, far more imprison-
ments, with countless beatings, and often near death. Five times I
received at the hands of the Jews the forty lashes less one. Three times
I was beaten with rods. Once I was stoned. Three times I was shipwrecked; a night and a day I was adrift at sea; on frequent journeys,
in danger from rivers, danger from robbers, danger from my own
people, danger from Gentiles, danger in the city, danger in the
wilderness, danger at sea, danger from false brothers; in toil and
hardship, through many a sleepless night, in hunger and thirst, often
without food, in cold and exposure. (ESV)

Yet despite all those difficulties Paul was completely content with just having Jesus.

Our job as men is to understand that God has given each of us unique
abilities to lead, serve, and do good things. So, yes, we need to work hard and
compete to the best of our abilities. That is what God wants us to do with the
talents He's given us.

But we will all go through some tough and trying times in our lives. Even though most of us will never go through anything like what Paul did, we all face adversity on some level. The question is, Can we still operate in contentment?

- Can we do our best in our relationships and know that God is in control and His plan is perfect?
- Can we stick with our jobs, even when they're difficult, and daily be content?
- Can we be content in our sports, hobbies, and other pursuits knowing that, win, lose, or draw, God has a plan and purpose for each one of us?

Jesus is enough for us. We find our contentment in Him. If we can get to the place of pure contentment in Jesus no matter what, then we will be able to do all things through Christ who strengthens us!

I (Colt) would say that this truth is the number-one thing God has been teaching me since my senior year in college. As of the writing of this book, have I accomplished everything I set out to accomplish in football and in life? The answer is no. Not even close. But I truly believe that in the end, if God doesn't let any of my dreams come to fruition, Jesus is enough.

We started out this chapter talking about wisdom, about welcoming trials because, in time, they make us "perfect and complete, lacking in nothing" (James 1:4, ESV). Contentment is proof that we've entered into that wisdom.

> We all face adversity on some level. The question is, Can we still operate in contentment?

Our lives may be turbulent, but our hearts are steady because they are fixed on the Rock. Comfort, achievement, and recognition all recede in importance, and what's clearer than ever in our focus is Christ and the unshakable salvation He gives us.

One more thought just before we close this book. Faithfulness to God is only applicable during the length of days we have here on earth. After we die and get to heaven, faithfulness won't be an issue. We'll be in the direct presence of God, the old things of this world will be passed away, and everything will be made new.

When it comes to faithfulness, we want to finish life on this earth well. Now, some may define finishing well as being the guy who dies with the most toys, or with a huge building with his last name on it, or having his name written down in record books as the guy who finished first.

But the true win in this area involves something you may not have expected. In fact, it's the exact opposite of living to be remembered, as we'll see next.

What You Leave Behind

We leave our best legacy to posterity when we focus on being faithful to God.

Have this mind among yourselves, which is yours in Christ Jesus, who, though he was in the form of God, did not count equality with God a thing to be grasped, but emptied himself, by taking the form of a servant, being born in the likeness of men.

—Philippians 2:5–7, esv

In October 2010, the University of Texas awarded me (Colt) a great and unexpected honor. They officially retired my number 12 jersey, which means that no other Longhorn can ever wear this number—forever. Only five other football players in the history of the school have had their jerseys retired, so I understood I was joining a select group. Quite frankly, the award surprised me. I felt grateful, and a good sort of pride welled up in my chest. It also got me to thinking.

In the sports world, the term *legacy* has specific connotations. It's all about your statistics and accomplishments. But apart from my jersey being retired and other achievements I've made in football, what legacy am I leaving?

If you've begun to mature in Christ, I bet the same question has occurred to you as well.

A lot of men's books end with a call to leave your legacy, meaning it's important to leave your mark on the world. But that's not what we want to do here. In that sense, "legacy" is equated with something important and significant that you created and that people will remember you by.

> In the sports world, the term *legacy* has specific connotations. It's all about your statistics and accomplishments.

To be honest, I do want to leave a strong legacy in the football world, in the sense that I want the way I play to reflect the excellence of almighty God. But that kind of legacy is not what redefining winning God's way is all about. There's a better kind of legacy you can focus on, a different sort of legacy that we want to invite you to create in this world—and it has nothing to do with being remembered. And if there's one thought we could leave you with as we close this book, it would be this:

Your true legacy actually has everything to do with being *forgotten*.

What's Your Calling?

Count Ludwig von Zinzendorf, a German church leader who lived in the mid-1700s, wrote and taught extensively, worked with orphans, established communities of faith worldwide, and penned a large number of hymns, many of which are still sung today. Today, he's credited with being one of many revivers of the Lutheran Church. If anybody could be credited with working toward being remembered, it could be Count Zinzendorf.

Instead, he wrote these words: "Preach the gospel, die, and be forgotten."[1]

That's it! That's the true kind of legacy we're talking about. Do what matters most in life. Finish your life. And don't worry about being remembered for who you were or what you did. The focus is not on you or your legacy; the focus is always on Christ.

Sure, it's a process to learn what that means for you. Many of the struggles I (Matt) have experienced in life stem from my wanting to perform, wanting to be known, wanting to be successful, and wanting to create a sermon that people will really love. But I've gotten to the place where that's changed. Today, for instance, when I'm preparing for a sermon, I'm focused on doing the best I can to the glory of God. I don't care much about getting positive strokes for myself anymore. I want to see people's lives changed, period—which is the whole point of bringing people together with God's Word. I'm going to be faithful to what God is calling me to do. I'm going to preach the text. And I'm going to trust God with the results.

Jesus once told men who were inclined to be proud of what they accomplished:

> When you have done all that you were commanded, say, "We are
> unworthy servants; we have only done what was our duty." (Luke
> 17:10, ESV)

The Lord Himself set the pattern for our selflessness, focusing on faithfulness to His Father. In the following description of Jesus by the apostle Paul, look for the images of His *letting go,* of His *emptying Himself,* of His *humbling Himself.*

> Have this mind among yourselves, which is yours in Christ Jesus, who,
> though he was in the form of God, did not count equality with God a
> thing to be grasped, but emptied himself, by taking the form of a
> servant, being born in the likeness of men. And being found in human
> form, he humbled himself by becoming obedient to the point of death,
> even death on a cross. Therefore God has highly exalted him and
> bestowed on him the name that is above every name, so that at the
> name of Jesus every knee should bow, in heaven and on earth and under
> the earth, and every tongue confess that Jesus Christ is Lord, to the
> glory of God the Father. (Philippians 2:5–11, ESV)

I'm sure that when Jesus died on the cross, it didn't look like He'd left much of a legacy. He'd written no books and accumulated no wealth. His reputation had been trashed by the authorities. The crowds had disappeared and His remaining followers were ready to scatter and go back to what they had been doing before.

But because Jesus had been faithful, God would create the greatest legacy ever out of that, a legacy that reaches to heaven, across the earth, and under the earth.

And note above all verse 5, which says that we are to have this same mind—this determination to be selflessly faithful to God—among ourselves.

That's what a true legacy looks like. Trust God and leave the results up to Him. A peace emerges from there. The legacy is not about your name being carried on; it's about the things that matter being carried on. In the long run, it's not about being remembered. It's about being faithful to your calling.

That begs the question: What is your calling?

We're going to offer three main areas that encompass every man's calling. The specifics will look different for each man, but the main areas will be the same. Think of these main areas as broad brush strokes that paint a picture for us of a true kind of legacy.

Your calling is to live in such a way that you leave a true legacy. It's to…

1. Be a city on a hill.

How do you leave a true legacy? In part, it's by living every day as a "city on a hill." The phrase comes from Matthew 5:14–16, where Jesus tells those who are following Him this:

> You are the light of the world. A city set on a hill cannot be hidden. Nor do people light a lamp and put it under a basket, but on a stand, and it gives light to all in the house. In the same way, let your light shine before others, so that they may see your good works and give glory to your Father who is in heaven. (ESV)

In other words, we are not called to live some sort of hidden, solitary life where people don't see us and don't know we follow Christ. To the contrary, we are called to live in the real world with all sorts of people from all sorts of backgrounds and faith persuasions. Our call is to live in such a way that the light of Christ shines before other people.

College football teams are not necessarily known as being groups that discuss Jesus Christ a lot. But in my (Colt's) days at UT, a few guys and I would often get together and have a Bible study. One day we were studying this passage in Matthew 5, and one of my buddies was like, "Dude, I heard this term— *COAH*. It stands for City On A Hill. That's what I want to be like."

We asked him to expand on what he meant.

He explained how he wanted to live differently. He didn't want his identity to be based on the fact that he was a Texas football player. He wanted to be a leader for Jesus.

We thought that sounded right on. It wasn't anything huge, but we started calling each other COAHs. It was a reminder to ourselves that we had an ability to be examples and role models. It wasn't a title to be anything more than we were, to act as if we were better than anyone else. Football is huge in Texas, so this title helped remind us to remove any swagger that might be present in our lives. We were Texas football players, sure, but that wasn't the core of our identity. We wanted to set the standard and be the light God wanted us to be.

> He explained how he wanted to live differently. He didn't want his identity to be based on the fact that he was a Texas football player.

Our football team didn't have a chaplain at UT, but as time went on, this group of guys who met together developed into a good core group to represent Christ. We'd pray together and hold Bible studies. Other guys started joining us.

One night after practice, we were meeting, and the subject of baptism came up. Lots of guys had different opinions, and a few guys had just started studying the Bible and had no idea what they were talking about. So we dived into the Scriptures and started figuring out what it meant. We came to the conclusion that baptism is a great thing, and that we're all encouraged to be baptized as Christians. I'd been baptized when I was fourteen, and it was an awesome experience.

So that same night after practice, five guys said they wanted to be baptized—and right away! There was a pool around the corner from the facility, so we went over there, and I baptized all five of those guys that night. It was an amazing night. By no means was it due to what I did or didn't do. It was the Holy Spirit working through the experience that softened hearts. These guys gave their lives to Christ and wanted to be fully submissive to what He wanted them to do, and so we baptized them.

> **That's what being a COAH means.... To be a city on a hill.**

When we talk about leaving a legacy, experiences like that are what it's all about. Sure, my professional role today is about being a quarterback in the NFL, but my life is also about so much more. I want to be the best Christian man and husband I can be. And I want to be the best role model and example I can be—whether I'm on or off the field. Everything I do, I want to do to the glory of God.

That's what being a COAH means. It's the calling of every Christian man. To be a city on a hill means you reflect God's excellence and glory in every area of your life. It's not so you'll be remembered after you die. It's so you'll live for what matters most. That's leaving a true legacy.

Meanwhile, the second way we can live to leave a true legacy is to...

2. Be a firmly committed family man.

Scripture is clear that our battle is not against flesh and blood (Ephesians 6:12). And I (Matt) have never seen any attack come against my life the way it did when I began to live out God's specific calling in my life. For me that meant planting a church. Today, more than ten years after starting the church, I've concluded that one of the main areas of attack that the enemy wages against your life, if you are married, will be against your marriage and your family.

Why? Why would the enemy attack your marriage and family? Because it doesn't matter what you do or accomplish in your job or in your ministry if, at the end of your life, your wife and children can't say, "He practiced in our life together what he claimed to believe."

Awhile back I read a fascinating book called *Good Christians, Good Husbands?* This book compares the marriages and families of three ministry leaders of the eighteenth century: John Wesley and his wife, Molly; George Whitefield and his wife, Elizabeth; and Jonathan Edwards and his wife, Sarah. It discusses how each ministry leader viewed his role as husband and father alongside his role as pastor.

John Wesley, the famous Methodist preacher, did some awesome things in ministry. In many ways he was a world changer. But when you pull back the curtains on his relationship with his wife, you see at once that the guy totally blew it in that area. He preached publicly that a husband and wife were to have a close relationship, but his own marriage with his wife, Molly, has been described as "the worst mistake of John's life."[2] Catch that? On the outside, everything looked great. But in reality their marriage was a wreck!

What in the world was going on between John and Molly? To her discredit, Molly didn't share her husband's calling to ministry and resented it when he was gone. (Remember what we said about a wife contributing to her husband's calling in chapter 7?) And to his discredit, John frequently corresponded with other women in ways that seem less than innocent and pure.

- To Dorothy Furley he wrote: "Write to me as often and as fully as you please."
- To Ann Ford he wrote: "How is it that you make me write longer letters to you than anyone else?"

- To Peggy Dale he wrote: "I thought it hardly possible for me to love you better than the last time I came to New Castle. But your artless, simple, un-disguised affection exceedingly increased mine."
- To Nancy Bolton he wrote: "O Nancy, I want sadly to see you. Your last visit endeared you to me exceedingly. Don't think of sending anything to me; except your love…it is sufficient!"
- To Sarah Ryan he wrote: "Sarah, I can hardly avoid trembling for you!"[3]

Scripture is absolutely clear—you've got to be a one-woman man. And emotionally, at least, or so it seems, John Wesley wasn't.

John Wesley's marriage eventually dissolved after thirty years. Molly left him and vowed never to return, so John was technically deemed the "innocent" party in the marriage and permitted to continue in ministry. Yet their marriage was tragic by many definitions of the word.

And theirs was not the only one.

George Whitefield had an enormous impact on thousands of people and is considered one of the greatest gospel preachers in all of history. Thousands of people responded to his messages and became Christians, and his influence reached the young, the old, the poor, the rich, and the influential.

He was also a man of integrity. When women wrote to him, he responded with absolute purity. One woman wrote him and was too affectionate, so he wrote back, "I only fear that you have my person too much in admiration. If you look to the instrument less, and to God more…it will be better."[4] In this, he was showing better judgment than Wesley had.

But here was the problem with George Whitefield. He loved his wife, Elizabeth, but he wasn't a very good husband. Whitefield viewed marriage as a means to an end, and he viewed his wife as someone whose whole purpose was to help him endure in his work. His own writings show that he viewed marriage only as a necessary hindrance to what he thought was really important: the ministry. He loved his wife, but "it was Whitefield's ministry that would have his heart."[5]

Elizabeth was a godly woman who loved George, but listen to this sad statement about their marriage: "With respect to her earthly husband, she lived as a 'widow.'"[6] Would your wife say something similar about you—that she loves you, but your work or your hobbies or your dreams truly have your heart? Tonight, ask your wife if sometimes she feels like Elizabeth Whitefield. If she says yes, then something needs to change in a big way.

That leads us to the last example of marriage: Jonathan Edwards and his wife, Sarah. Edwards accomplished much in ministry, but what's more amazing is how he was successful both in ministry and as a family man. He viewed no separation between his calling as a pastor and his calling as a husband and a father. He lovingly pursued his wife, spent time with each of his children, and instructed his family in the Lord.

His daughter Esther recorded in her journal,

Last eve I had some free discourse with my Father on the great things that concern my best interest. I opened my difficulties to him very freely and he as freely advised and directed. The conversation has removed some distressing doubts that discouraged me much in my Christian warfare. He gave me some excellent directions to be observed in secret that tend to keep my soul near to God, as well as others to be observed in a more public way. *What a mercy that I have such a Father! Such a Guide!*[7]

Who among us wouldn't want our daughter or son to say that of us? And Edwards's wife, Sarah, had equally great things to say about her husband. After Edwards died, his wife wrote his daughter a letter.

Oh my very dear child, what shall I say? A holy and good God has covered us with a dark cloud. [God] has made me adore his goodness that we had your father so long, but my God lives and God has my heart. Oh what a legacy my husband and your father has left us.[8]

That's the line to leave burning in our ears. *Oh what a legacy my husband and your father has left us.* Again, the point is not so you'll be remembered after you die, even in a good way, even by the people who matter most in your life— your wife and children. It's that you'll live for what matters. That's leaving a true legacy.

Let those three examples guide us. Two marriages, John Wesley's and George Whitefield's, show what not to do, one through emotional entanglements with other women and one through neglect of his wife for the sake of ministry. One marriage, Jonathan Edwards's, shows a man who was firmly committed to his family, not only his career. What will your family say about you?

And then the third way we can live to leave a true legacy is to…

3. Be courageous in fulfilling your specific calling.

All of us as men have a general calling: to follow Christ wholeheartedly in both private and public and, if we are married, to be firmly committed family men. But what of a specific calling? This is the calling that only you can do. God designed you with a specific purpose in mind. Colt's is to be a professional football player. Matt's is to be the pastor of a large church. What's your specific calling?

The answer that many men give is that they're not sure. And this is okay, at least for a while. It often takes time for a specific calling to emerge and then to be shaped and confirmed. One afternoon Colt was talking to me (Matt) about what he might do after his career in football was finished. Most men in the NFL have about a ten-year shelf life, tops; then they need to move on to something else. Colt talked about opening a sports camp one day, but even then he was unsure.

I challenged him to seek the Lord's will above all else and to dream big. God has gifted Colt in ways He hasn't gifted almost anybody else on earth. I mean, he's one of only about thirty-two people out of a population of more than six billion on earth who can do what he does in his career. But then again, isn't that the way it is with all of us? We're all gifted in unique ways. Our callings are not the same, and that's the wondrous part of God's plan in our lives.

Leadership circles talk about the BHAG, which stands for Big Hairy Audacious Goal.[9] It's the ultimate thing you could do or achieve if there were no hindrances in your life. In many ways God gives us all BHAGs, dreams and goals that seem unattainable at first. And the goals *are* unattainable—unless we have faith. The key with a spiritual BHAG is that it's got to be for the glory of Jesus, period. If our BHAG is anything else, it's a waste of time.

> Our callings are not the same, and that's the wondrous part of God's plan in our lives.

Take something as career defining as winning the Super Bowl. If that's your only goal in life, when you finally attain it you'll discover at that moment, if you haven't already, that there has to be more to life. Your achievement will actually create disillusionment, not contentment.

That experience of disillusionment can be helpful, though. Why? Because it points us back to the eternity God has placed in our hearts. Nothing can satisfy us except Him. Not even winning the Super Bowl. It sounds counterintuitive, but that's what the real win is all about. Whatever your goal is—maybe you just won the Super Bowl or you have more money than you know how to spend or everybody knows your name—you're still not content. That's the way life works. Unless God is in your heart, you're going to be asking yourself, *Why in the world did I do this?*

So how do you create a specific calling?

Well, you don't. It's something God places in your life. Yet you can still position yourself to know it and respond to it when the time comes. Make sure you're working for the Lord. And make sure you're working for eternal values. We'll be giving a few more tips below.

For a long time, I (Matt) never wanted to be a pastor. When I was younger,

I wanted to be a doctor. But eventually I sensed that God wanted me to go into full-time vocational ministry and preach. For some time I fought that call because, honestly, I didn't want to be poor.

One summer between my sophomore and junior years of college, I was working for a construction company in Texarkana and driving back to Dallas every chance I could to see my future wife, Jennifer. One afternoon on the freeway I was praying, wrestling with God, and not wanting to surrender or do what He was asking me to do. Then a Christian song came on the radio. It was cheesy, but it was powerful to me. One line went, "Will you be the one to answer to His call?"[10]

> That was my moment of surrender.... I laid down my will and picked up His, whatever His will was.

I sensed the Lord was speaking to me. I pulled over by the side of the road and prayed, "Lord, I don't care where You want me to go or what You want me to do. I'm Yours, and I'll do whatever You want." That was my moment of surrender. I stopped wrestling. God had brought me to the place where I laid down my will and picked up His, whatever His will was.

That invitation is held out to you as well. Whatever God's specific call is on your life, come to a place of surrender.

We see examples all the time of men responding to God's specific call in their lives. Awhile back at Austin Stone, a man retired after a fruitful career in business. He was senior vice president of a large computer company and had spent his whole life doing what he needed to be doing—loving his wife and family, going to church, and working well. After the man retired, he faced a choice: go live in Florida and do nothing much, or ask God if He had anything else for him to do.

The Lord captured his heart. The man sensed that God was inviting him to do more with his life. So he sold his eight-thousand-square-foot house in Austin, bought some duplexes in one of the poorest neighborhoods in Austin, and moved into one of the units himself. He lets single mothers and under-resourced families live in the other duplex units for free while they get back on their feet. Meanwhile, he and the other members of his small group from our church serve and help the people living in these duplexes as needed. It's been amazing to see how God is working in that neighborhood.

Do you sense God is inviting you to a specific calling? What might you need to do? It might not be to become a pastor or to buy a string of duplexes. But there is some goal that looks big, hairy, and audacious—and God is calling you to step forward. What do you do?

- *Inquire.* Begin by asking yourself: *Am I living for myself, or am I living for the Lord?* If you're living for the Lord, that's awesome. If you're living for yourself, then pray for transformation and take steps in that direction.

- *Surrender.* Stop wrestling with God. Get to that place where you say, "This is not about me, Lord, it's about You, and I'll do whatever You want me to do." You might not know what you need to do, but you get to the place where you're willing to do whatever's required of you.

- *Prepare.* If you sense that the Lord may be calling you to a specific place, you might want to take classes in that area first, or read books, or build up reserves, or learn a new skill, or hone an existing skill, all in preparation for launch.

- *Wait.* Wait actively and expectantly, with great faith. Psalm 46:10 encourages us to "cease striving and know that I am God" (NASB). Only God knows what will happen to you after that. Your story is being written by Him, as you follow His lead. You don't have to figure out your vision. God is going to reveal it to you.

- *Launch.* Put your seat belt on. When God says what your specific calling is, then you go. You're obedient. You're courageous. You're fully following God.

One Single Passion

Pastor John Piper wrote something that illuminates what we're after when we think about creating a legacy that leaves us forgotten and God famous. In his book, *Don't Waste Your Life,* he lays down a series of unforgettable challenges:

> God created us to live with a single passion: to joyfully display his supreme excellence in all the spheres of life. The wasted life is the life without this passion. God calls us to pray and think and dream and plan and work not to be made much of, but to make much of him in every part of our lives....
>
> Desire that your life count for something great! Long for your life to have eternal significance. Want this! Don't coast through life without a passion....
>
> But whatever you do, find the God-centered, Christ-exalting, Bible-saturated passion of your life, and find your way to say it and live for it and die for it. And you will make a difference that lasts. You will not waste your life.[11]

That's what we're talking about. The point is not living so you'll be remembered after you die. It's living for what matters. That's leaving a true legacy—and God's definition of the real win redefines what we live for. Too many men live their lives in vain. They walk about like phantoms, making uproars for meaningless causes, amassing riches for purposeless things, or lazing on the sofa eating potato chips. But life passes by far too quickly, and when we gain a sense of the limited number of our days and what truly matters in life, we will live with a new urgency.

> The real win means trusting the Lord, walking with Jesus, and living your life in the way He defined it.

God's call to you is to live your life with unction, a calculated abandon that places God at the center of all you do. The real win means trusting the Lord, walking with Jesus, and living your life in the way He defined it.

Will you be a man who redefines winning God's way for the rest of your life?

Remember, the real win is built on two simple but strategic commitments— who we trust and who we serve. Those two decisions change everything for a man. When we trust and serve God wholeheartedly, we can be absolutely confident, no matter what life throws at us. It doesn't matter ultimately if we're successful in the eyes of the world or not. It doesn't matter ultimately if we fulfill our goals or not. In Christ, our hearts are satisfied.

Will you join us in this quest today?

The Winner

We've been talking about the real win in this book—living our lives according to God's plan through trusting and serving Him. Meanwhile, along the way, we've been skirting an idea that it's now time to bring out fully. You see, not only is there a real win, one that's different from what we would choose for ourselves out of our limited and selfish perspective, there's also a real winner, and that's not us.

That's God.

Step back for a moment. Way back, so that you're no longer focusing just on your own life and the lives of those you touch. In the grand historical scheme of things—from the garden where Adam first set us men off on our course of struggle with masculinity, to the distant future long after we've fulfilled our legacy of being forgotten—God is working to bring His perfect plan to completion. And we know from the book of Revelation that Christ will be the conqueror on a white horse, heaven will come to earth, and all things will be made right...forever.

God is the great Winner, and so it is only appropriate that we live our lives to magnify His glory, as John Piper reminded us in the last chapter. And it only makes sense that we subject our own limited plans for ourselves to whatever plans God has for us. Because as we take our small yet important part in His grand plan, we become a part of the greatest victory of all and experience all the fulfillment that we could ask for. Therefore, we can give up our worries about whether we're doing things right as men, and whether the outcome will be what we want, because we can have confidence that the victory we are a part of is 100 percent assured.

So be a real winner on the side of the great Winner.

- *Win at home.* Be a leader in your family by loving your wife first and seeing that she and your kids are following the Lord.
- *Win with your work.* Quit making an idol of worldly success in your job and instead work as for the Lord.
- *Win in your character.* When you're tempted, turn to Jesus for help. If you fail, repent and receive God's grace and mercy.
- *Win the future.* Accept the shaping influence of God through the trials in your life, and determine that, whatever comes, you will live the rest of your life to establish His glory rather than your own.

If a quarterback and a preacher from Texas can find authentic success in God, you can too. We're excited to think about all God is going to do in your life and, through you, in the lives of many more around you.

Trust in the LORD *forever,*
    for the LORD GOD is an everlasting rock.
    —Isaiah 26:4, ESV

ACKNOWLEDGMENTS

Matt: I'd like to thank Marcus Brotherton, Jordan Bazant, Travis Wussow, David Kopp, and Stephen Crawford. It would have been impossible to write this book without all of you. I would also like to thank elders, staff, and partners of The Austin Stone Community Church. Partnering with you for the sake of the Gospel has been one of the greatest joys of my life.

Colt: I'd like to thank my wife, Rachel; my parents, Brad and Debra; and Jordan Bazant.

STUDY GUIDE

If my team and I (Colt) were to listen to our coach telling us about the game plan, agree that it sounded great, and then proceed to forget all about it, next Sunday's game would look pretty ugly! We've got to actually carry out what we learned if our play on the field is going to be any good.

The same goes for this book. Matt's and my greatest fear about this book is that you'll read it, nod along with the points you like—then do nothing about it. That's the *real loss* we're worried about. And so we created this study guide to help you come face to face with how our teaching in *The Real Win* applies to you. Because that's what really matters: Not just reading about trusting God but actually trusting Him. Not just wishing you had a life built on the Rock but actually having one.

For each chapter, we've provided a brief review and a handful of questions to read on your own or discuss with others. You'll find that for every chapter there's at least one question that gets you digging into a Bible passage, since, after all, it's the Word that's the ultimate source of the wisdom you need to live a faithful life. Feel free to look up more Bible passages and add to or adapt our questions, to tailor the study experience for yourself and anyone else you're using this guide with.

Use this study guide:

- in a men's small group
- at a men's retreat
- with a male friend you trust
- with your wife or fiancée
- on your own

Whatever setting you choose, you will need to decide how to use the content. For example, you can use this study guide in eleven separate sessions, one for each chapter. Or you can follow a five-session format like this:

- Session 1: Introduction to the real win (chapters 1–2)
- Session 2: Winning at home (chapters 3–5)
- Session 3: Winning at work (chapters 6–7)
- Session 4: Winning in your character (chapters 8–9)
- Session 5: Winning over a lifetime (chapters 10–11)

Over and over again through the years, Matt and I have each benefited in huge ways from talking honestly with other men about Scripture and about our lives. Recently, Matt has also been my spiritual coach—and *The Real Win* is one of the fruits of the great mentor-learner relationship we've enjoyed together. As you discuss the issues in our book with some other men, you'll grow into the trusting, secure relationship with God you need most.

Let's get started. It's game day!

—Colt McCoy

Chapter 1: Transformed by Trust

So many men start out to win what they most want but in the end don't get it. Or they think they're achieving what matters most, but in the long run, life doesn't pan out the way they'd hoped. What happens then?

If we're truly going to succeed, we need to redefine success. The real win for a man is built on two simple but strategic components—who you trust and who you serve. Those two decisions change everything for a man.

The task isn't always easy, but the rewards pay off in big ways. With God at the core of your life, your life is rock-steady. A peace and assurance like you've never felt before flood your life. You know that by trusting God, you're living out your life in the center of His perfect plan.

1. What do you want in life more than anything else?

2. Have you begun to be disillusioned by your pursuit of some worldly goal? If so, explain.

3. In the midst of his cancer ordeal, Matt received advice from a friend about living with *unction*—holy urgency. Read Psalm 39:4–5, the passage Matt read at that time. Would you say that you are living with unction? Why or why not?

4. Just as Matt learned to trust God through cancer, Colt learned the same lesson through losing a college football championship game. What events in your life have taught you the most about trusting God?

5. In his interview with Lisa Salters after the championship loss, Colt said, "God is in control of my life, and I know that if nothing else, I am standing on the Rock." Read Isaiah 26:3–4, the passage Colt had in mind as he spoke those words. How do you think your life might be different if you were standing on God the Rock in absolute confidence?

Chapter 2: Achievement vs. Faithfulness

We men are born to strive, to compete, to shoot for success. But as we pursue our goals, things can go terribly wrong. We start out to win the way we want to win, but in the end we lose in what really counts. Or we think we're achieving what matters most, but along the way we end up losing what we actually value.

The real win means trusting the Lord and walking with Jesus no matter what. That kind of faithfulness is possible for any man who follows God with all his heart. No matter what circumstances threaten him, a faithful man is the most truly confident man in the room.

1. In what areas of your life do you feel most driven to achieve? How has achievement failed to give you the satisfaction you expected?

2. What are the idols in your life? In other words, what do you pursue more than you pursue God?

3. Read Ecclesiastes 3:11. This verse says that God has planted within everybody a longing for the stuff that really matters—the stuff that's eternal. When and how have you felt this longing for eternity?

4. In chapter 2, the authors say,

The drive to achieve is natural and good, if handled appropriately. But it isn't everything. It isn't why God put you here. Instead, the Bible shows us a higher value. The questions become: Are your eyes on Jesus? Are you faithful to His calling? Are you doing your best and leaving the outcomes to God?

What are your answers to these questions? Give reasons.

5. If you made faithfulness to God a higher value in your life than achieving worldly success, what things would have to change? What might be the benefits for you in the long run?

Chapter 3: Willing to Lead

The Scriptures are clear that God has placed a calling on men to lead. We're not to be passive. We're not to shift responsibility to others when it's ours. The Bible teaches that we are to take leadership in our businesses, churches, communities, and especially our closest relationships—with wives, girlfriends, children.

So *how* do we discover how to lead?

By trusting in Jesus. He's the only man who lived a perfect life. He died on the cross, was raised in power, and now lives in us and gives us the ability to walk boldly through life and look more and more like Him as we live our lives.

1. Do you think of yourself as a leader? Why or why not?

2. Give an example of a time when you know you didn't lead as well as you should have.

3. Read Genesis 2:15–17 (God's one prohibition to Adam) and Genesis 3 (the story of Adam's failure to lead his wife to obey the prohibition). How do you relate to Adam's passivity?

4. Colt and Matt identify several sins of failed male leadership:
   - The sin of acting macho
   - The sin of materialism
   - The sin of anger
   - The sins of dominance and control
   - The sins of laziness and immaturity
   - The sins of emotional and spiritual absence
   - The sins of spiritual legalism and hyperspirituality
   - The sins of hedonism and frivolity
   Where do you see yourself in this list? Give examples.

5. How has Christ helped you to become a better leader? In what areas do you still need to improve?

Chapter 4: Love Her First

In our marriages we lead by taking the initiative to give our wife what she needs most—our love. And that's so even if she isn't giving us everything we'd like. Almost always, a man's taking leadership by loving his wife *first* leads her to eventually reciprocate by giving him the respect he craves. But whatever a wife's response may be, the husband's responsibility is to be faithful to God's call upon him in this area and to lead with love.

1. What evidence have you seen that women love to be pursued?

2. Read Ephesians 5:21–33, a key passage in the Bible about marriage. How does Christ serve as a husband's example in this passage?

3. If you have not been doing a good enough job in taking the initiative to show love to your wife or girlfriend, what's holding you back?

4. What are your wife or girlfriend's preferred love languages? With these love languages in mind, how can you show her love in ways that she'll notice and appreciate?

5. Matt says he gives himself up for his wife, Jenn, by taking strict precautions to maintain sexual purity. Colt says he gives himself up for his wife, Rachel, by spending time with her even when he's tired after work. If you are married or seriously dating, what does it mean for you to give yourself up for your wife or girlfriend?

6. What are some first steps for you to take the initiative in your relationship and love your wife or girlfriend?

Chapter 5: Rev. You

At church we've got a pastor looking out for our family's spiritual well-being. But at home we need to make sure that our wife and kids are growing toward Christ all the time. In effect, we're the pastor at home.

Here's truth—as men, it's *always* our responsibility to lead in spiritual matters. Although we might not know how, it's up to us to learn how.

1. What have you done well as the spiritual leader in your home? What have you done poorly?

2. Review the passage you looked at for the previous chapter: Ephesians 5:21–33. Note especially verses 26 and 27 that speak about Christ sanctifying the church. If you are married, how are you being a leader by helping your wife grow toward greater sanctity or holiness?

3. If you are married, what practical steps have you found to be most helpful for being the spiritual leader in your marriage? If you are single, in what ways could you appropriately lead your girlfriend in spiritual matters?

4. Read Deuteronomy 6, where God gives parents the responsibility to pass on their spiritual heritage to their children. What principles does this passage teach that are still relevant to parents today?

5. What practical steps have you found to be most helpful for being the spiritual leader to children?

6. What can you do to keep on improving in your skills as the "pastor" in your own home?

Chapter 6: What You Care About Most

Idolatry. God placed an injunction against it as the very first of the Ten Commandments. And idolatry is still a serious problem today, with serious implications. Idolatry occurs anytime we take something and place it ahead of God in our hearts.

It's not easy to root out the idols of our hearts, to confess them to the Lord, and to walk forward in true success. But it's God's call on our lives.

1. Read Exodus 20:2–6, the beginning of the Ten Commandments. Why do you think it is such a big deal to God that people not try to put anyone or anything in His place?

2. Colt and Matt say, "An idol is anything a man pursues more than he pursues God." What is the idol that you are still struggling with most? Why do you think it has such a hold on you?

3. Read Mark 2:1–12. The paralytic in this story thought his greatest need was to be healed, but really his greatest need was for forgiveness of his sins. Keeping your idol in mind, how would you complete the following sentences?

   • What I think is my greatest need: _____.

   • What really is my greatest need: _____.

4. Matt and Colt identify four major idols in men's lives:

   • The idol of power
   • The idol of control
   • The idol of comfort
   • The idol of approval

   Discuss how one or more of these idols is a problem for you.

5. God removes an idol from a man's life in one of two ways: by *withholding* what a man wants or by *giving* him what he wants. Either way, it leads to a man's understanding that what he wanted was of less importance than he previously thought. In which of these two ways—withholding or giving—has God removed an idol from your life? (Maybe He's in the process of doing it right now.)

6. What's your role in getting rid of the idols in your life?

Chapter 7: Choose Your Boss

Work is something we'll do most of our lives. So how can we find purpose, joy, and value in the work God has called us to do? The answer is, we're to work for God and not for men.

Each of us is to be serving the Lord and not our earthly boss. We should trust in Him and look to Him to direct us into what He wants us to accomplish with our gifting, our time, and our energy. If we do that, it's a win no matter what anybody else might say.

1. What do you do for a living? How do you like it?

2. Read Genesis 2:15 (describing Adam's job in the garden) and compare it with Genesis 3:17–19 (describing how Adam was cursed in his work life). How do you feel the same work-is-what-I'm-meant-to-do-but-work-is-just-so-darn-hard tension in your life?

3. Read Ecclesiastes 2:4–11, 17–26. What can you relate to in Solomon's musings about his work experience?

4. Colt and Matt offer three pieces of advice for men who are living in a fallen world and yet who are experiencing the redemption of Christ. They say…

- Whatever work you do right now is God's will for you in this moment. Embrace it.
- Whatever you do, work heartily, as for the Lord and not for men.
- Wherever you work, you can find purpose and joy and value in your work when you understand that you are where you are because God has placed you there.

  Which of these pieces of advice do you need to most take to heart right now, and why?

5. If you are married, how does your wife already come alongside you in your calling? And how might the two of you arrange things so that you become even stronger partners? If you are single, what kind of wife do you need to look for to partner with you in your calling?

Chapter 8: The Voice of Temptation

How does a man seek the real win in times of temptation?

The answer is not to trust in our willpower. Again the answer is to trust in God. If we'll turn to Jesus, He has the power to help us say no to the temptation and avoid the sin. And that's always better than having to recover from the sin after giving in to it!

1. How would you define *temptation*? How would you define *sin*? Give an example of where you think a person crosses a line between temptation and sin.

2. If you're willing to share them, what temptations are you struggling with most right now?

3. Read Hebrews 2:10–18 and 4:14–16. What does it mean to you personally that Jesus understands your struggles with temptation?

4. Would you agree with the authors that when it comes to resisting temptation, trusting in Christ is superior to trusting in your own willpower? Why or why not?

5. Matt and Colt give four practical strategies for relying on Christ in the face of temptation.

- *Use the Word of God*—read and memorize Scripture and bring it back to mind when tempted.
- *Talk to God about your temptation*—pray for God's strength to resist temptation.
- *Love God*—focus on raising the level of your affections for Christ, because this will lower the attraction of sin for you.
- *Stay in your lane*—organize your life in such a way as to avoid some temptations.

   Take each one of these pieces of advice in turn and discuss how you *are* following it or *could* follow it.

6. How could your friends help you persevere in resisting temptation?

Chapter 9: The Welcoming Arms of God

What do we do when we have fallen short of God's high moral standards for us? And what can we expect His reaction to be?

Winning God's way does not have to be over for us when we've made a mistake. If we're trusting in Him, God has a way of welcoming us back from our detour and putting us back on the path to living in a way that fulfills His beautiful plan for us. He's got grace and mercy waiting for us the minute we return to Him.

1. When you've sinned, how do you think God feels about you?

2. If you're struggling with sin (and who isn't?), Colt and Matt advise you to try to get to the root cause of the sin, because then you can see why you are going to something other than God for satisfaction. Answer the following two questions to get at the root cause in your own life. (Note that it may take a lot of praying and thinking before you can answer the second one.)

   - *Where* do you sin?

   - *Why* do you struggle with that surface sin?

3. How would satisfying yourself with Jesus make you less interested in satisfying yourself with the junk of the world?

4. Review some verses you looked at in the previous chapter: Hebrews 4:15–16. How is God showing you grace and mercy today despite your moral failures?

5. Where would you say that you stand today in your battle against sin? Still needing to understand your motivations for sin better? Needing to ask forgiveness of God and turn from sin? Needing to accept God's grace and mercy and go on in your life through faith? Or what?

Chapter 10: Hard School

Difficulties in life often make us wonder where God is. Is there any greater purpose for the difficulty? Can God accomplish anything good through the hard time? Or are we experiencing this trial all for nothing?

Scripture says we can actually welcome trials with joy if we recognize that they lead to endurance and that this endurance in its turn leads to spiritual maturity.

You see, for the believer, trials produce wisdom. And wisdom is more valuable than just about anything. Through wisdom we learn to be content with what God is doing in our lives, even if it isn't what we wanted, because we trust Him and His greater plans for us.

1. How have hardships taken you off the path toward the win you wanted in your life? How have those same hardships put you on the path toward the win God wants for you?

2. Read James 1:2–8, a passage that turns our worldly response to the trials of life on its head. How have your trials led to endurance? How has this endurance led you nearer to spiritual completion?

3. What is an example of some of the wisdom you have picked up from the suffering in your life so far?

4. How are your present troubles affecting your faith in God and God's plan for good in your life?

5. Read Philippians 4:10–13. Could you honestly repeat Paul's words about being content whether brought low or abounding in good things? Why or why not?

6. What do you still need to do to incorporate the hardships of your life into your quest for authentic, godly success?

Chapter 11: What You Leave Behind

When most people think about leaving a legacy, they think about doing something that will cause them to be remembered after they're gone. But a man's true legacy actually has everything to do with being *forgotten*.

We are to trust God and live for what matters, then leave the results up to God. A peace emerges from there. The legacy is not about our name being carried on; it's about the things that matter being carried on. In the long run, it's not about being remembered. It's about being faithful to our calling.

God's call to us is to live our lives with unction—a calculated abandon that places God at the center of all we do. The real win means trusting the Lord, walking with Jesus, and living our lives in the way He defined them.

1. According to Matt and Colt, a man's legacy should be to make God famous and be forgotten himself. What is your reaction to that idea?

2. Read Philippians 2:5–11. What does Christlike humility look like in the life of a man? How does this humility contribute to accomplishing the will of God in a man's life?

3. What opportunities do you have to leave a legacy by being a "city on a hill" for God?

4. If you are a committed family man, how will this contribute to leaving a godly legacy?

5. What is the specific calling God has placed on your life? How will fulfilling that calling help you to leave a godly legacy?

Final question:

6. How will you live differently after studying *The Real Win*?

TALKING TOGETHER FOR A CHANGE
Colt and Matt explain the mentoring process.

As you've seen in the pages of *The Real Win,* the authors' friendship is deeply rooted in a years-long mentoring relationship. But how does mentoring actually work in practical terms between two people—one a teacher, one a student?

We asked Matt and Colt to share some of what they've learned together over the years.

Typically, mentoring describes a process where a senior or more experienced individual agrees to help a younger, less experienced person learn and grow. The relationship might focus on personal disciplines, faith, relationships, work, and career. For Matt and Colt, it encompassed all of those. And the outcome was life changing for both men.

Describe how the mentoring relationship actually works between you?

Matt: Our mentoring relationship began during Colt's days in college. Throughout Colt's senior year, we met once a week in my office. That time was spent looking through Scripture, praying together accountability, and discussing any issues that Colt was facing at the time. The topics we discussed ranged from answering theological questions that his teammates were asking him, to how to walk in purity with his girlfriend. At times, Colt needed a pastor— someone to teach him the proper course of action in a given situation. In other areas, Colt needed a friend—someone to walk with him through the pressures and fears any young man faces as he walks through life. As the years have gone by, our relationship has turned more from a mentor/mentee relationship into a friendship or peer relationship. Many times now, Colt is the one doing the ministering, teaching, listening, and counseling.

Colt: I remember a time where I was struggling with knowing how to love my wife well. My wife loves quality time with me. That means turning off the TV and really connecting through conversation. She wants to feel like she has my complete attention. Well, I was exhausted from a long season of football, and all I wanted to do after I got home from practice was to sit on the couch and unplug. Matt reminded me that while it's okay to allow myself some time to unplug after work, ultimately as a man and a husband, I am called to love my wife well. Of course, I wanted to do that, but how? We spent some time thinking through what that could look like. Then we developed a practical plan that helped me put her needs first and love her in a way that ministered to her.

Colt, what would you say are the primary benefits of having a mentor?

Wisdom. Nothing can replace experience and the wisdom that comes from that experience. Countless times I have gotten on the phone and had a question for Matt because of a challenge I'm facing. He speaks into those situations because, more often than not, he has already walked through them. Even when he hasn't, he is able to offer helpful biblical insight. To have a person in my life whom I can count on to give me godly counsel in those situations is priceless. Regardless of what situation I'm going through, to have men like my father, my grandfather, and my pastor to lean on and glean from their wisdom has been invaluable to me through the years.

Matt, who do you consider a good candidate for mentoring?

Two of the characteristics that attracted me to Colt were that he was teachable and had a hunger to grow. It has been my experience that many young men seek out mentoring relationships as a one-sided exchange. Here's what I mean: they approach an older man to mentor them with the expectation that they are going to simply *absorb information*. Colt not only listened to what I taught him, but he was always *committed to do* what it took to implement those principles we talked about during our times together. This made our conversations so much more meaningful and fun. And I knew that Colt's commitment meant he would act and things would likely change.

Colt, looking back, how has your life been affected by Matt's investment?

It's hard to measure, but so many aspects of my life have Matt's fingerprints on them. Whether I am preparing a message for a chapel service for my football team or simply have a question about my marriage, Matt has been a steady source of help and encouragement to me. The highest compliment I could give my mentoring relationship with Matt is that I love Jesus more today because of our time together.

Matt, what have you learned from your relationship with Colt?

Honestly, being in a mentoring relationship with Colt has been one of the most rewarding experiences of my life. To see Colt grow from a kid in college with the weight of the world on his shoulders to a grown man leading his wife, his family, and his teammates in the pursuit of the Lord is rewarding beyond measure. I have learned from Colt that when a man sets his mind to growing and maturing in the Lord, it is going to happen.

Does mentoring ever happen in surprising circumstances?

Colt: One conversation I'll never forget happened on a hunting trip that Matt and I were on together. Others have happened while we're fishing. We try to schedule time to do something together that we both love, and inevitably our best conversations are simply an overflow of that time.

Matt: Exactly. As Colt points out, mentoring relationships really do work best when the two people involved are "doing life" together. That means many of our conversations with the most impact have happened in a duck blind, a deer stand, a bass boat, or around the barbecue in the backyard. Yes, we've had great conversations in my office, but I have tried to involve Colt in the natural rhythms of my life, family, job, and recreation. As we have spent time together in these everyday settings, growing together has been the natural result.

Matt, as a pastor, what else would you recommend to men to who are thinking of becoming mentors?

First, you don't have to be a pastor or some other kind of "professional" Christian to mentor younger men. The most powerful thing you have to offer someone you are mentoring is your life, and the wisdom and experience you've learned from it.

And second, just be the man you would want to be mentored by. Be available, be honest, be vulnerable. Give him access to your life. The results will be more rewarding than you can imagine.

NOTES

Preface

1. For more about Colt's life and the latest news in his career, go to ColtMccoy.com. You can see Matt's interview with Colt at www.youtube.com/watch?v=B0rEfQIFBjE. You might also want to read Colt's autobiography: Colt McCoy and Brad McCoy, *Growing Up Colt: A Father, a Son, a Life in Football* (Urhrichsville, OH: Barbour, 2011).
2. To learn more about the church where Matt is the pastor and where Colt worships when he's in Austin, check out Austinstone.org.

Chapter 1: Transformed by Trust

1. You can watch Colt's postgame interview with Lisa Salters at www.youtube.com/watch?v=o5XdrLCftsY.

Chapter 2: Achievement vs. Faithfulness

1. Joseph Stowell, *Simply Jesus and You* (Colorado Springs: Multnomah, 2006), 23–24.

Chapter 3: Willing to Lead

1. Ryan Murphy, "Wheels," *Glee,* season 1, episode 9, directed by Paris Barclay, aired November 11, 2009.
2. We're indebted to Mark Driscoll for his teaching in this area and for helping us think through these concepts.

Chapter 4: Love Her First

1. Gary Chapman, *The Five Love Languages* (Chicago: Northfield, 2009). In case you're interested, Dr. Chapman has also published a men's edition of this best-selling book.

Chapter 5: Rev. You

1. Sally Lloyd-Jones, *The Jesus Storybook Bible: Every Story Whispers His Name* (Grand Rapids, MI: Zondervan, 2007).

Chapter 6: What You Care About Most

1. We're indebted to Tim Keller and his teaching on idolatry and the story of the paralytic in the book of Mark. His writings have helped greatly in our thinking through the concepts presented in this chapter.
2. Joseph Stowell, *Simply Jesus and You* (Colorado Springs: Multnomah, 2006), 33–35. Used with permission.

Chapter 7: Choose Your Boss

1. Andre Agassi, *Open: An Autobiography* (New York: Knopf, 2009), 3.
2. Social media is currently vying for second place.

Chapter 11: What You Leave Behind

1. John Wesley, *Journal* (London: Robert Culley, n.d.), 2:11. http://countzinzendorf.ccws.org.
2. Doreen Moore, *Good Christians, Good Husbands? Leaving a Legacy in Marriage and Ministry* (Ross-shire, Scotland: Christian Focus Publications, 2004), 23.
3. Moore, *Good Christians,* 43–44.
4. Moore, *Good Christians,* 89.
5. Moore, *Good Christians,* 93.
6. Moore, *Good Christians,* 93.
7. Moore, *Good Christians,* 106.
8. Moore, *Good Christians,* 126–27.
9. James Collins and Jerry Porras, *Built to Last: Successful Habits of Visionary Companies* (New York: HarperBusiness, 1994), 113.
10. Al Denson, "Be the One," *Be the One,* Benson Records, 1990.
11. John Piper, *Don't Waste Your Life* (Wheaton, IL: Crossway, 2003), 37, 46–47.

ABOUT THE AUTHORS

Colt McCoy is currently a quarterback in the National Football League. He was the winningest quarterback in the history of NCAA football and led his University of Texas team to the 2010 BCS National Championship game. During his senior year, Colt won thirteen of the top fifteen major college player awards, including quarterback of the year, offensive player of the year, and outstanding football player of the year. The 2008 Heisman trophy runner-up, Colt has been involved in domestic and foreign ministries. During the off-season, he and his wife, Rachel, live in Austin, Texas. For more information, see ColtMccoy.com.

Matt Carter is the lead pastor at Austin Stone Community Church. Planted in 2002, the church has grown from a core team of fifteen to more than eight thousand regular attenders today. Matt graduated from Texas A&M and holds a master's degree in divinity from Southwestern Seminary, where he is currently pursuing a doctorate of ministry. He speaks at conferences and seminars around the country. He and his wife, Jennifer, live in Austin with their three children. See AustinStone.org.

About the Collaborative Writer

Marcus Brotherton is a journalist and professional writer known internationally for his literary collaborations with high-profile public figures, humanitarians, inspirational leaders, and military personnel. He is the author or coauthor of more than twenty-five books, including the *New York Times* bestselling *We Who Are Alive and Remain,* with twenty of the last surviving Band of Brothers. See www.marcusbrotherton.com.